Powerful Places

in

Malta

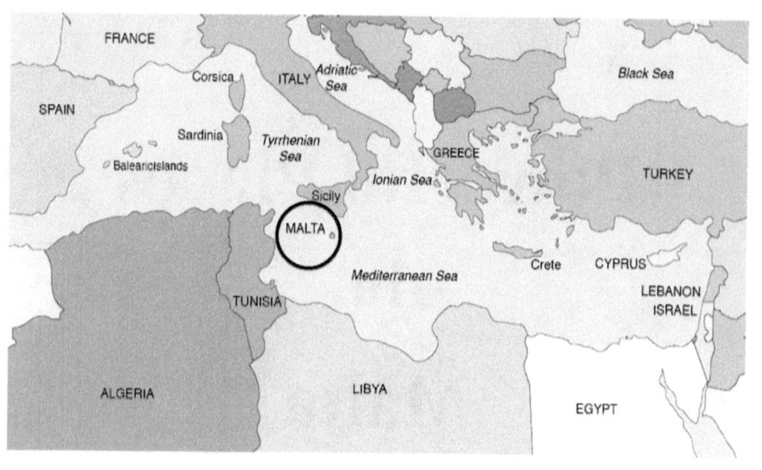

FRANCE
SPAIN
Corsica
ITALY
Adriatic Sea
Black Sea
Sardinia
Tyrrhenian Sea
Balearic Islands
GREECE
TURKEY
Sicily
Ionian Sea
MALTA
Crete
CYPRUS
Mediterranean Sea
LEBANON
ISRAEL
TUNISIA
ALGERIA
LIBYA
EGYPT

Powerful Places
in Malta

A Broader Perspective

Elyn Aviva

&

Gary White

Powerful Places in Malta

A Broader Perspective

by

Elyn Aviva & Gary White

ISBN: 978-0-9915267-8-9

Set in Adobe Text Pro 11 pt. and Myriad Pro in various sizes.

Cover photo: Inside Mnajdra South Temple, Malta, photo by Elyn Aviva

Photo Credits: Elyn Aviva, Adobe Stock, Google Earth, and AncientOrigins.com (p. 73)

This book is dedicated with gratitude

to the Spirit of Malta.

Contents

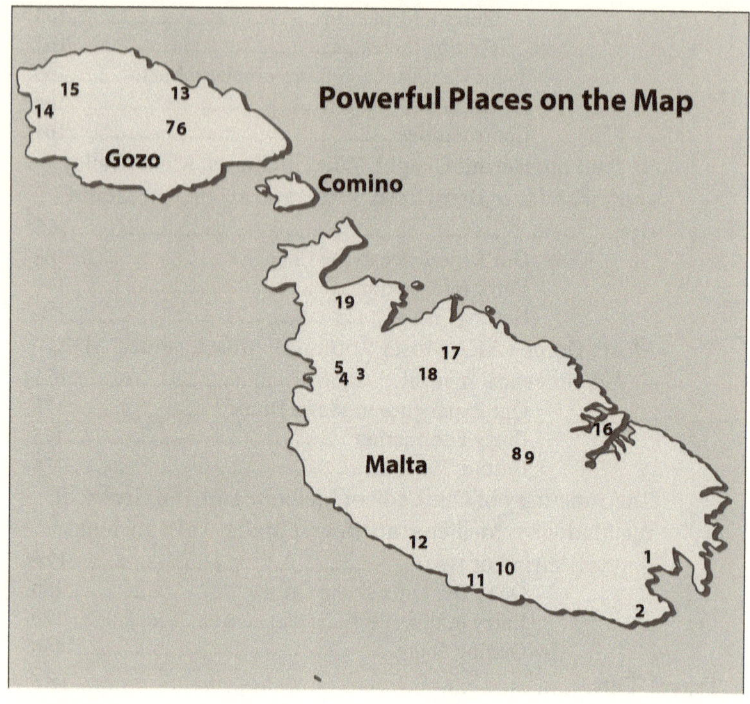

15
13
14
76
Gozo
Comino
Powerful Places on the Map
19
17
5
4 3
18
16
8 9
Malta
12
1
11 10
2

Why this Guidebook is Unique

Over the years, we have written a series called Powerful Places Guidebooks, dedicated to sacred sites and powerful places.[1] Since we kept returning to Malta, we were often asked whether we would write a guidebook about it. Our answer was always a resounding "NO!" Although we knew there are many powerful places scattered across the two main islands of this Mediterranean nation, we also knew that the theories, hypotheses, stories, etc. about them are plentiful and incompatible.

After our last visit to Malta, however, we suddenly had a revelation. It is precisely because there are so many conflicting stories that we needed to write this Powerful Places Guidebook. People deserve to know about the disparate explanations and contradictory assertions.

This is not your usual travel guide, filled with superficial facts and summary descriptions. Instead, we provide context and background information for specific powerful places and, equally importantly, a number of alternative interpretations and perspectives. Nor do we attempt to describe every worthwhile place to visit on Malta. We concentrate on locations from the prehistoric period because they are where the controversies swirl and because many of them are powerful places. We include a few historical sacred sites and places of natural beauty, of which Malta has an abundance. We also offer brief accounts of some of our experiences at selected sites.

Here are various questions we will be exploring:

Was Malta really first settled 8,000 years ago by Sicilian farmers?

Did these farmers suddenly start to build unique, massive limestone temples—without precedent and unlike anything found elsewhere in the world—around 6000 years ago?

Why did they build so many? Surveys indicate some 66 megalithic temples existed on the relatively small islands of Malta and Gozo.

What is the relationship between the Maltese temples and the sun, moon, and stars?

Based on "obese" statues and the interior layout of the temples, some people believe Malta was the site of a Mother Goddess cult. But are the large-bottomed, kilted statues (often headless) always female, and are the temples proof of a Goddess cult?

Some archaeologists state that Ħal Saflieni Hypogeum, an underground construction that resembles an above-ground temple, was a huge cemetery into which some 7,000 (decomposing) bodies were deposited. But was it?

Numerous limestone plateaus are covered with networks of enigmatic cart-ruts that run parallel, overlap, do "U-turns," and even go down the sides of cliffs and under the water. How old are they and what were they used for?

We present different explanations and viewpoints. Due to new evidence and shifting scientific interpretations, the dates in this guidebook may at times be internally inconsistent and may not agree with other online information or published books.

In addition, as an archaeologist friend reminded us, "Everybody has an agenda." And everybody has unconscious biases. This includes archaeologists, museum curators, alternative-history theorists, New Age channelers, and tour guides—and the two of us, Elyn and Gary. We have tried to be balanced and objective in our presentations, providing a range of theories and (often) the difficulties they present. When we have a definite opinion, we state it.

Sometimes "fact" and "truth" are the same. Sometimes there is a difference. "Truth" may be based on an inner awareness that sometimes offers a more meaningful and richer explanation. "Fact," on the other hand, while it may seem objective and unbiased, is often highly selective and based on incomplete information.

Throughout this guidebook, we encourage you to do further research, examine the facts, draw your own conclusions, and/or follow your intuition to discover which explanations ring true to you.

We provide three appendices: a pronunciation guide, a list of archaeological phases, and a glossary.

Powerful Places

As in the other books in our Powerful Places Guidebooks series, we provide background information about a number of carefully selected sites, how to get to them, and, often, a brief narrative describing our own experiences at these powerful places. We also give suggestions that can turn casual tourism into transformational encounters.

> "In the universe, there are things that are known, and things that are unknown, and in between, there are doors."
> William Blake

We are often asked, "Just what is a powerful place?" Based on our extensive experience, we define a powerful place as a place that feels—different. A place where you feel unexpectedly energized, serene, a little spooked, joyful, covered with goosebumps, deeply grounded, very uncomfortable.... You get the idea. Powerful places are found all over the world in nature: on mountaintops and inside caves, in forests and deserts, beside the ocean and on the banks of a river. Powerful places include battlegrounds and the birthplace of a holy person. Powerful places are also intentionally created at special locations by humans using sacred geometry, astronomical alignments, and knowledge of Earth energies. These sacred sites include stone circles, dolmens, shrines, cathedrals, and temples.

How do you experience a powerful place? The brief answer is, by centering, grounding, and being attentive to a site in whatever way works for you. Much of the time we humans operate "on automatic," hardly registering where we are or what we feel. Visiting a powerful place is an opportunity to be intentional, conscious, mindful, and alert. In order to fully experience a powerful place, it is important to be aware of your surroundings and of subtle changes in yourself in response to the environment.

Feeling the subtle energies in a place requires sensitivity and intuition. It is a bit like tuning a radio dial to a particular frequency. We didn't feel much at powerful places until we started studying with geomancers and dowsers. Acquiring the techniques of dowsing and other avenues to the sensing of earth energies is outside the scope of this guidebook.[2] But we will provide some suggestions, from our experiences, of how you can "attune" yourself to the powerful places we describe. Of course, every person has within them such capabilities, and you may find a completely different path to awaken them.

When approaching an ancient, human-constructed sacred site: 1. Remember the site puts us in contact with the people who built it—not directly, but through the monuments themselves. People constructed them thousands of years ago. That's amazing. It's a kind of "time travel." 2. Explore the uniqueness of the site. Our ancestors expended a great deal of effort constructing it. Pay attention to the stones, the sacred geometry, and the underground energies that you may be able to sense. 3. Enter into relationship with the place as if it were an animate, conscious being. Communicate with it; "connect" with it. And, 4. Notice the Mystery: nobody really knows what anything really is.

Before entering a church, temple, or tumulus—or certain natural sites, such as an old-growth forest—pause a moment. Ask permission from the spirits, the ancestors, or the guardians of the place. Imagine that you are entering someone's home or place of worship: you wouldn't simply barge in without asking, and you would want to be polite. If you sense a positive response before entering a sacred site, place your hand lightly on the standing stone or doorframe to the right of the entryway. Attune yourself (come into energetic harmony) with the place. Then step over (not on) the threshold, if it is safe to do so.

It's not always easy to be centered and attentive to a place, especially at a popular tourist destination—which many of the places described in this guidebook are. In addition, many powerful places and sacred sites are "managed" in such a way as to almost prevent you from having a meaningful experience. A chattering guide or audio earphones takes your attention away from being present and keeps you in your head. Such diversions encourage you to look but not to see. This can be frustrating, so just remember the acronym **BLESSING**.

BLESSING stands for: **B**reathe slowly and regularly, paying attention to your breath moving in and out. If you have a breathing practice, now is the time to do it. **L**ook and **L**isten within: what are you sensing internally? How do you feel? **E**stablish yourself in your location, perhaps by orienting to the seven directions (east, south, west, north, above, below, and the center within; or, before you, behind you, to your right, to your left, above, below, and the center within). **S**ense your surroundings, opening your five (or six) senses to what is around you. State your **IN**tention to respect this place and to experience what is present. **G**ive gratitude for this opportunity.

> Malta is a very powerful place, and certain locations sometimes have destabilizing energies. Maybe that's because the islands are limestone, and water percolating through the limestone through millennia has caused numerous underground cracks, crevices, and caves. Maybe it's because that same process causes a subtle electric current to flow through the land at different places. We have also found many of Malta's sacred sites are full of surprisingly powerful energies, each with its unique "flavor" and worth savoring—if you resonate with that particular "taste."

We encourage you to listen carefully to your own inner guidance as you open yourself to a powerful place on a particular day, at a particular time of day, with the particular predisposition you bring to that moment. You must use your own judgment to determine what is good or not good for you. Trust your feelings. Leave if a place doesn't feel right; stay if it feels good. And always, enjoy the mystery.

Introduction to Malta

The Republic of Malta is an archipelago composed of three main islands (Malta, Gozo, and tiny Comino), a number of diminutive, uninhabited islets, and several large rocks that rise out of the sea. The largest island, Malta, is only 17 miles long and 9 miles wide; Gozo is only 8.7 miles long and 4.5 miles wide. Comino is 1.4 sq. miles in area.

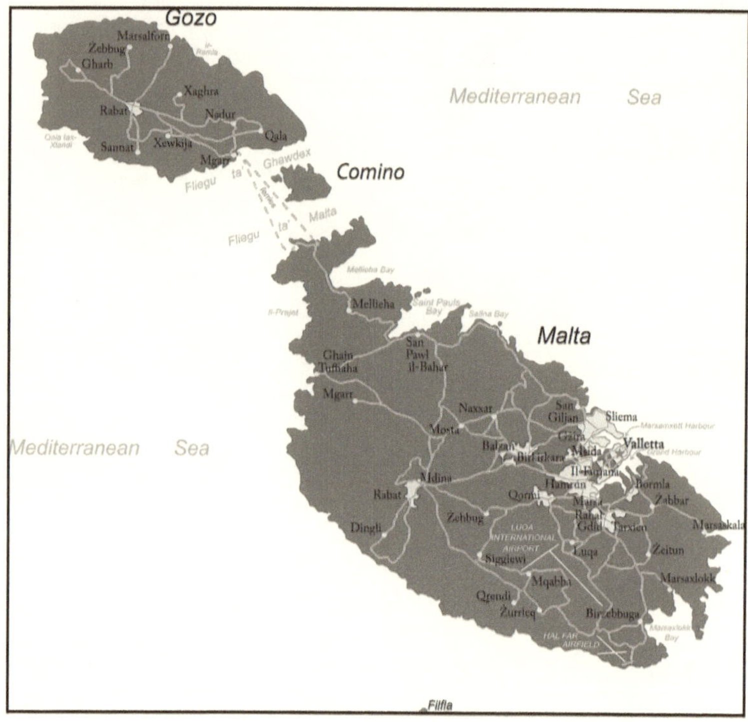

The Republic is usually referred to as Malta. It is located at an important crossroads of the Mediterranean, just 50 miles south of Sicily, to which it was once attached by a land bridge, 180 miles east of Tunisia, and 217 miles north of Libya.

It is the smallest (122 sq. miles) member of the European Union and is densely populated: 475,000 people live on the three populated islands. Nearly 440,000 of them live on Malta, 33,000 on Gozo, and 10 on Comino.

The Flag of Malta

The economy revolves around tourism; film production; electronics, pharmaceutical, and textile manufacturing; and maritime-related activities, such as freight trans-shipment. Artisanal products include hand-made lace, silver filigree, indigenous-bee honey production, leather work, and blown glass. The people are predominantly (94%) Roman Catholic and very devoted to their village saints and exuberant religious festivals called festas.

The official languages are Maltese (the national language) and English. Maltese ("Malti" in Maltese) is a unique, Semitic-based language written in Latin script. (See Appendix 1 for a pronunciation guide.) Maltese is the only Semitic official language in the European Union. It has a complex linguistic history, with roots going back to an extinct form of Siculo-Arabic that developed in Sicily and was introduced into Malta between the 11th and 12th centuries. The language has been heavily influenced by Sicilian, Italian, some French, and English. Phoenician was also spoken on the island several thousand years ago, and Punic (a form of Phoenician) inscriptions have been found. At one point it was thought that Maltese may have derived from Phoenician, but modern linguistic investigations do not support this theory.

Recent genetic analysis indicates that modern Maltese are the very mixed and hybridized descendants of Sicilian and Calabrian colonists who repopulated the islands beginning in the 10th or 11th century. There is little evident genetic input from North Africa. It appears that the previous inhabitants—including the Phoenicians, Romans, and Byzantines—were decimated during the Arab conquest by the Aghlabids in 870 CE. However, some highly disputed (probably not credible) research suggests Phoenician ancestry lives on in Maltese men's genes, if not in the Maltese language. It is puzzling how Phoenician genes (or language) could have survived on Malta since the islands were depopulated for nearly 200 years, beginning in the late 9th century. At any rate, the islands are not just a geographical crossroads but also a cultural and linguistic mélange.

Prehistory of Malta

The islands were formed some 30 million years ago from compressed sediment. At some point they were submerged under what is now the Mediterranean Sea and then pushed up again. The archipelago lies on the underwater ridge called the Maltese Plateau. It is all that remains of what was once a land bridge linking Malta to Sicily, Europe, and North Africa during the last Ice Age. At one time, the sea levels were as much as 120–130 meters lower. Malta gradually became isolated as the sea level rose at the end of the last Ice Age, approximately 10,000–12,000 years ago.

Before the land bridge was submerged, animals (and perhaps humans?) traveled across it. 200,000-year-old animal fossils have been discovered in the lowest levels in Għar Dalam Cave. Some of these animals (hippopotamuses and three species of elephant) exhibit island dwarfism and are related to animals found in Africa; others (the giant dormice and giant swans) exhibit island gigantism and were native to Europe. Island dwarfism is caused by animals adapting to food scarcity and the lack of predators on small islands; gigantism is caused by the absence of predators and, perhaps, the opportunity to become predators of smaller animals.

Why these animals became extinct is unknown. Such extinction often is linked to the arrival of humans, but no remains of early human habitation during that epoch have been found on Malta—or rather, what evidence may have been found has been seriously challenged and even, perhaps, tampered with.

The islands are composed of uneven layers of sedimentary rocks: Coralline and Globigerina Limestone, Blue Clay (blue-gray mudstone), and Greensand (a kind of sandstone). The greyish Coralline Limestone is, in general, harder and more difficult to work than the honey-colored Globigerina Limestone. Both types of limestone were used in constructing the massive Maltese temples.

Malta is characterized by low hills, farmland (olive trees, dairy production, some vegetable farms), rugged cliffs, stunning coves, alternating valleys and ridges, and numerous natural harbors. There are no rivers and only limited freshwater supplies. The islands are also subject to flooding events and earthquakes, which have resulted in the alternating valleys and ridges as well as in the deposit of fossils and debris in caves and cul-de-sacs.

Human Prehistory on Malta

Archaeologists have divided Malta's prehistory into 11 phases, named after the sites where datable or sequential material was first discovered. This can be a bit confusing for laypeople, so we have often substituted dates for phases. (See Appendix 2 for a list of the archaeological phases.)

There is much disagreement about when humans first arrived on Malta. Most archaeologists assert that the earliest human occupation occurred during the Neolithic era (see Appendix 3 for the glossary), after the end of the last Ice Age. As you will see later in this guidebook (p. 24), there are many tantalizing hints and artifacts that suggest that people arrived much earlier on the islands—in fact, during the last Ice Age. This topic is hotly debated.

For decades, most publications have stated that the earliest date of human settlement on Malta was ca. 5200 BCE (Before Current Era). However, the most recent (2018) multi-disciplinary analysis by Queen's University of Belfast archaeologists, based on material found at Xagħra Stone Circle on Gozo, asserts that Malta was populated 700 years earlier than previously thought and experienced several waves of colonization.

According to Prof. Caroline Malone, head of the research project, people settled in Malta around 5900 BCE. Their DNA indicates they came from different parts of the Mediterranean, Europe, and Africa. They lived in open-air villages like the one excavated near Skorba (see p. 33), and inside natural caves like Għar Dalam (see p. 17). They were farmers and introduced domesticated animals and pottery of a kind known to have originated in southeastern Sicily. These settlers began building small, one-room stone temples or shrines. Several are found at Skorba, and one contained fragments of several female figurines that may have been connected with worship of a Mother Goddess or Goddess of Fertility.

The Queen's University researchers propose that these first settlers drastically degraded the soil through poor farming practices. Along with extended drought, lack of food resources eventually forced them to leave. Or perhaps they died out. The islands were then uninhabited for 1000 years.

A second wave of colonization arrived from Sicily around 3850 BCE and lasted 1500 years. These were the people of the so-called "Temple Period," which is generally agreed to have begun around 3600 BCE. Within 200 years after their arrival, these Neolithic farmers began building unique, massive, multi-room megalithic temples, complete with carved decoration of impressive artistry. Their building tools included stone hammers, chisels, obsidian and flint blades made from imported materials, and antler picks. They had no metal. These temples are now acknowledged to be among the oldest free-standing structures yet discovered—older than the Great Pyramid, older than Stonehenge. Seven of them have been named UNESCO World Heritage Sites.

Where did the inspiration come from? That's a very good question! It seemed to come out of nowhere and began within only a few hundred years after these subsistence farmers settled on Malta.

Anthony Pace states, "Elsewhere in the ancient world, nothing comparable was being built in stone in lands located within a short distance from Malta. Nearby Sicily appears to have remained oblivious to Malta's megalithic phenomenon, in spite of contacts and sea travel. The same can be said of Sardinia and the Italian mainland."[3]

There is no evidence of warfare during these early prehistoric times. Trade with neighboring regions included the importation of flint and obsidian (a shiny black volcanic glass), alabaster, pottery styles, and ochre (red iron oxide). The obsidian was used for tools, the alabaster for figurines, and the ochre for coloring temple walls and decorating special stone blocks, statuettes, and skeletal remains. Ochre has been used since the Paleolithic era in burials and in rock art.

The burial practices of these early people changed over millennia. Originally, the dead were buried in natural caves and rock-cut tombs. Over time, individual tombs gave way to successive, perhaps familial, burials in the same space. These required a kind of primary and secondary burial; older bones were pushed back to make room for the more recently deceased. In later centuries, the preferred burial practice appears to have been to construct a much larger and impressive communal chamber. This "cemetery" probably also included secondary burial—the redisposition of bones after the body had decayed—along with grave goods. Xagħra and Ħal Saflieni Hypogea are examples.

According to Prof. Malone, the peaceful Temple Period people mysteriously disappeared around 2350 BCE, possibly due to radical climate change and severe drought. Tree-ring data from 2354 BCE shows clear evidence of extreme climate change in the region, perhaps caused by a vast volcanic eruption, or a meteor, or comet dust or debris in the atmosphere blocking out light. Legends throughout the world describe a time of flood, darkness, unusual clouds, and general turmoil. The "4.2 Kiloyear BP aridification event" that began around 2200 BCE affected much of the northern hemisphere.

Torrential storms may have washed soil down the hillsides, making farming even more difficult. Vegetation also became much sparser. Rain alternating with drought may have made it impossible for the ancient Maltese to survive. They may have died from starvation; they may have emigrated to what they hoped would be a more agriculturally productive land.

Several centuries later, perhaps around 2100 BCE or perhaps a few centuries earlier, the islands received a new population. These people were members of a completely different, Bronze-Age culture. They used copper weapons, cremated their dead, and built smaller, cruder megalithic structures called dolmens (see Appendix 3: Glossary).

It's possible this was not a new population but rather the same population with a totally different social and cultural organization, the result of some unknown but natural progression. However, this explanation seems highly unlikely.

Soil erosion and major faulting events, social upheaval, centuries of more and less inept "archaeological" digs, modern unbridled land development, and political/nationalist/academic pressures have all contributed to the challenge of determining what really happened during the prehistory of Malta. It is difficult to find undisturbed skeletal or cultural remains, and hence there is a lack of adequate, datable material with which to construct an accurate timeline. The recent multi-disciplinary work by Queen's University of Belfast is rewriting what people thought they knew about prehistoric Malta—or at least, about Gozo—but it is just a beginning, and their conclusions may be superseded in the future, just as previous scholarly conclusions have been superseded.

Historic Period on Malta

More than a millennium after the arrival of the Bronze-Age population, Malta entered the historic record via subsequent settlers, visitors, traders, raiders, and conquerors. These included the literate Phoenicians (800–218 BCE, although the Phoenician culture continued on Malta for many more centuries), the Greeks (settled on Malta around 700 BCE), the Carthaginians (480–218 BCE), and the Romans (took over in 216 BCE). St. Paul was shipwrecked there in 60 CE and introduced Christianity to the islands. Next came the Byzantines (4th to 9th centuries) and the Vandals and Ostrogoths (invaded in the mid-400s). In 870 CE, North African Arabs pillaged the islands and left them almost depopulated. Malta was recolonized by Siculo-Arab-speaking settlers from Sicily and Calabria in the mid-11th century. Then came Normans (Malta was part of the Kingdom of Sicily, beginning in 1091), the Spanish/Aragon/House of Barcelona (ruled from 1282–1409), the Sicilians, and the Ottoman Turks. The Holy Roman Emperor Charles V gave the islands to the Knights of St. John of Jerusalem, AKA the Knights of Malta, in 1530. And then, finally, the islands became the property of the French (1798–1800) and the British (1814–1964).

A Knight of Malta

The islands became partially independent from Great Britain in 1964 and a republic within the Commonwealth in 1974. In 1979 they became a neutral and non-aligned state. Malta joined the EU in 2005 and the Eurozone in 2008.

Prehistoric Sites on Malta

In this section on prehistoric sites in Malta, we will describe two caves that show signs of human occupation, a number of important ancient temple sites, and the enigmatic cart-ruts. We will also examine a number of the conflicts, controversies, and conspiracies that spin around Maltese prehistory like a whirlpool.

The Caves

Water percolating for millennia through the limestone layers of Malta has created numerous caves. Two of these—Għar Dalam and Għar Hasan—are especially significant for our exploration of powerful places on Malta.

Għar Dalam Cave and Museum, southeast Malta — Layers of life and death

Għar Dalam (pronounced aar-dalam) is located near Birżebbuġa (beer-zeb-boo-jah), in southeast Malta. The name is routinely translated as the "Cave of Darkness," but the name may be corrupted from Ghar Dalum (Cave of the Elephants) or refer instead to the surname "Dalam," hence, "Dalam's Cave." "Cave of Darkness," however, is much more evocative. The cave is famous for its stratified deposits of animal fossils and human artifacts.

The cave is located in the side of Wied Dalam, a now dry, rocky valley that leads down to the sea. Għar Dalam was formed over millions of years by water percolating through and dissolving the Lower Coralline Limestone hillside. Ancient flooding events washed numerous bones of animals into the cave, where they settled into uneven stratigraphic deposits.

The Għar Dalam Museum provides a variety of educational exhibits, including numerous skeletal finds, an unusual Victorian-style bone display, and human artifacts. The cave is accessed via a path that leads from the museum. Branches of the cave penetrate 475' into the hillside. The tunnel-like front part of the cave is approximately 164' long and up to 26' high. This section has been developed to accommodate visitors. It is well illuminated and easy to access. The rest is off-limits to tourists.

The cave was explored, with varied degrees of care and expertise, half-a-dozen times between 1865 and 1938. Excavations at Għar Dalam revealed a number of stratigraphic layers. There is disagreement about their number and ages, but we have tried to choose the most reliable sources.[4]

The first layer is the oldest and deepest, dating back to 500,000 years ago. It is a layer of clay, empty except for some plant impressions.

The second, perhaps dating back 200,000–180,000 years, is called the "Hippopotamus" layer and includes animals demonstrating island dwarfism and island gigantism, evidence of their long existence on a restricted land mass. Fossils in this layer include dwarf elephants—some of the size of Saint Bernard dogs; dwarf hippopotamuses; micro-mammals; and giant swans and dormice. It is thought that normal-size animals moved south over the land bridge between Malta and Italy to avoid the approaching ice of the last Ice Age, and they became isolated on the island due to rising sea levels.

Why they became extinct is unknown. It might have been due to human predation—but there is no indisputable evidence of human presence on Malta that early. One could reasonably assume, however, that Paleolithic hunter-gatherers followed the herds as they headed south. (Pygmy hippos on Cyprus went extinct when humans arrived on the island around 9000 BCE.)

Above this layer is the third layer, composed of small boulders and pebbles. This is evidence that a fast-flowing river flowed through the cave at some point.

The fourth layer is called the "Deer" or "Red Deer" layer and dates to around 12,000 years ago. The earlier dwarf and giant species have become extinct and have been replaced by red deer, brown bear, red fox, wolf, and vole. It is possible that humans "culled" the red deer population for food, but that would require a human presence on Malta earlier than the archaeologically agreed-upon consensus indicates.

Early excavation reports from 1917 indicate that human artifacts and remains were also found in this layer. Researchers found two molar teeth with taurodontism ("bull-teeth-ism") in 1917 and, in 1936, a third. Taurodontism (a marked degree of fusion in the roots) is a characteristic of Neanderthal teeth—which would be proof that people lived on Malta long before the Neolithic migrations. Subsequent analysis, however, seemed to prove that these teeth belonged to modern humans, not Neanderthals. (These results are subject to much debate in the "alternative" literature. For more on this controversy, see p. 24.)

The fifth layer is calciferous (containing calcium carbonate and, according to one report, volcanic ash).

The sixth layer, which is quite disturbed from previous digging, is known as the "Cultural" layer and dates from the Holocene period, approx. 12,000–10,000 years ago, according to one source; according to two other sources, this layer dates either from 7,400 or from 7,200 years ago. The latter date makes more sense since layer #6 is logically more recent than layer #4.

The remains discovered in this top layer are approximately 7,400 (or 7200)–2,700 years old, based on C-14 dating, and include domestic animals (cows, horses, sheep, and goats), worked flint, tools, ornaments, and pottery sherds.

The pottery style is similar to that created by farmers in Stentinello on the Sicilian coast at that time. This is a version of the widespread Impressed Wares that are found from Croatia to Spain. Apparently, the first settlers on Malta made themselves at home in caves as well as in open-air villages. Other sherds of different design were also found in this level, indicating much more recent habitation. The cave was used as a cattle pen until the initial dig in the mid 1800s.

In early 2019, excavations just outside of Għar Dalam resulted in a surprising find: animal bones and other archaeological artefacts, dumped there when excavations within the cave were conducted many years ago. Perhaps new evidence will surface there. Unfortunately, because the material is so thoroughly disturbed it will be difficult to establish credible dating.

Our Experience in Għar Dalam

Elyn's Experience: It was hard for me to ignore the controversy that surrounds the possibly Neanderthal teeth found in Għar Dalam, but I decided I would focus on the indisputable fact that very ancient people had lived here. It was also hard for me to ignore the "managed" appearance of the cave: the surfaced walkway, the handrails, the electric lights, the chattering of tourists, the labels placed here and there to indicate stratigraphy. I tried to concentrate on my breath, focus on my intention, and center myself, but it wasn't easy.

Eventually, by hanging back from the group, I was able—briefly—to sink into a reverie about what it might have been like to live in this cave. I appreciated the safety provided by this ready-made shelter—safety from wild animals and also safety from the heat of summer. I imagined families settling into their respective niches, perhaps sleeping on furs or piles of grasses. How convenient it all was. No need to gather building materials or do repairs when the roof leaked. What a comfortable, cozy place this was. I could almost smell the fragrance of earth and bodies and animal skins, almost see the flicker of smoky tallow lamps. As I walked deeper into the cave, the natural light faded, and I felt a sense of calmness and peace—despite the crowd and the artificial lights.

I remembered going into souterrains/fogous in Cornwall, underground constructions with long sloping narrow entry passageways that open into larger spaces and (often) alcoves. Although Għar Dalam was much bigger, there was something familiar, something similar—a journey ever-deeper into Mother Earth, from which we all spring and to which we all return....

Entry Information

Entrance to the museum and cave requires a ticket. Entrance is included in the Heritage Malta Multisite Pass. For more information go to http://heritagemalta.org. A path leads from the museum at the entrance to a 55-yard-long walkway into the cavern. There is also a garden planted with indigenous plants and trees.

Getting There

Għar Dalam and nearby Birżebbuġa can be reached by regular buses from Valletta. The cave and museum are on the right-hand side of the road at a small parking area, 1/3 mile before Birżebbuġa. Malta Sightseeing "Hop On Hop Off" South/Red Tour includes a stop at Għar Dalam. (See "Travel Tips," p. 181.)

Għar Hasan Cave, Southeast Malta — Disputed cave art

Għar Hasan (aar-hasan) is a limestone cave situated in the side of a precipitous cliff near Għar Dalam. The cave is accessed by descending 25 steps from the surface to a level walkway with iron railings, which leads across the cave face to the entrance to the cave. The cave branches off into several galleries, one of which descends about 100 yards to another opening in the cliff. Access is currently restricted to the first part of the cave. There is a spring inside the cave. A bat colony and woodlice, among other fauna, inhabit the cave.

Although no Pleistocene fossils or prehistoric artifacts have been found in the cave, the area around it is rich in prehistoric, Bronze, Punic, and Roman remains, including a menhir (see Appendix 3) and dolmens (see Appendix 3). Roman pottery sherds were found in a back chamber of Għar Hasan, which may have been used as a rock-cut burial site.

Folklore includes the legend of the Saracen Hasan, who is said to have hidden in the cave in 1122 when his people were expelled from the island. There are various stories told about Hasan, but the basic motif is that he kidnaps a beautiful young

Maltese girl and keeps her prisoner in the cave. She tries to escape. The story ends when either she and Hasan plunge to their deaths from the cave, or she stabs him to death while he sleeps and then escapes to her own village. Another legend says that the interior of Għar Hasan is so long that the tunnels reach the Grand Harbor region, some 5 miles away.

The importance of Għar Hasan lies not in its folklore but in its very old rock art. In 1987 a team of Italian archaeologists from Centro Camuno di Studi Preistorici, led by rock-art expert Prof. Emmanuel Anati, claimed to have discovered Paleolithic cave art in Għar Hasan caves. The red, brown, dark brown, and black designs were faint but visible, covered by a thin layer of minerals emanating from dripping stalagmitic formations, indicative of great age. The art depicted human hands, anthropo-zoomorphic (mixed human/animal) creatures, ideograms, and several animals, including elephants.[5] The photographs and drawings were donated to the National Museum of Archaeology. The archaeologist David H. Trump mentions the cave art briefly but discounts its significance.[6]

Getting There

There is no public transport to Għar Hasan, which is 1.6 miles south of Birżebbuġa. Access is restricted to the first part of the cave.

Controversies

As mentioned above, teeth that have been claimed to belong to Neanderthals have been discovered in Għar Dalam—which raises the contentious question of just when did humans arrive on Malta.

What's the Evidence?

Although human remains have been found on Sicily dating back to 24,000 BCE, in the midst of the last Ice Age, and Sicily was at that time connected to Malta by a land bridge, the archaeological consensus has been that there were no human inhabitants on Malta prior to the Neolithic settlers in 5200 BCE. As mentioned earlier, Queen's University research has now pushed that date back to 5900 BCE, but that's thousands of years later than the end of the last Ice Age.[7]

Contemporary archaeologists publicly express their desire for earlier dates, disappointment that nothing has been proven, and wistful hope that additional, verifiable evidence will be found. For example, Prof. Anthony Bonanno states, while discussing the land bridge that united Sicily to Italy and to Malta, "This means it was equally possible for contemporary humans (Neanderthals and, later, Anatomically Modern Humans) to reach and roam on these higher lands; hope persists among archaeologists that secure and stringent evidence of such activity will one day be unearthed."[8]

The archaeologist David Trump put it this way: "The fact remains, however, that despite early claims of 'Neanderthal' teeth from Għar Dalam, claims recently revived, and of Paleolithic cave art in Għar Hasan, and Clactonian and microlithic flints from various much later sites, there is no secure evidence yet for human settlement before the end of the sixth millennium BC, much though we should welcome it. We can begin our story safely only with the early farmers."[9]

Trump doesn't explain why he dismisses these claims. Presumably it is because of the questionable quality of the evidence.

These two archaeologists certainly sound eager to embrace earlier dates for human presence on Malta, but when one looks at the last 100 years of Maltese archaeology, one discovers a trend: the dismissal of intriguing data that suggests a much earlier time frame.

In an early publication, the renowned anatomist-archaeologist (Sir) Arthur Keith states that the teeth found in Għar

Dalam are clearly characteristic molar teeth of Neanderthal.[10] This interpretation was considered correct for a number of decades. By 1964, however, the idea that humans lived on Malta before the Neolithic was considered invalid. Nitrogen analysis of the teeth in 1952 and 1955 appeared to demonstrate they belonged to Anatomically Modern Humans (AKA Homo Sapiens). A number of scholars (David H. Trump and Nadia Fabri among others) are satisfied that these results are valid—but not all.

Dr. Anton Mifsud, a retired Maltese pediatrician and researcher, believes there are numerous problems with the previous analyses, including erasures in the original data records, incomplete release of information, and misrepresentation of the results.[11] Thanks to Mifsud's persistence, the age of the teeth is being reconsidered. According to a 2016 newspaper article, Aida Gomez-Robles, one of the leading London Natural History Museum experts whom Dr. Mifsud consulted, said in a letter she sent to Heritage Malta requesting access to the teeth:

"Based on this [her PhD research] experience, I can state that at least one of the teeth from Għar Dalam shows all the anatomical traits that are characteristic and exclusive of Neanderthal molars, which very strongly supports the Neanderthal classification of the individual to whom this molar belonged."

The report states that two other experts from the museum, Shara Bailey and Tim Compton, have also backed up Dr. Mifsud's findings. The next step would be to submit the teeth to DNA analysis. We have been unable to determine if this has been done. It appears that the teeth are in the possession of Heritage Malta, and at least in 2016 they appeared unwilling to send them out for external testing. If the tooth (or teeth) proves to be Neanderthal, this would push back the date of human habitation on Malta to (possibly) 35,000 years ago.[12]

The disputed analysis of the teeth is not the only example of what appear to be efforts to negate or discredit evidence of earlier human habitation in Għar Dalam and elsewhere on Malta.

As mentioned earlier, in 1987 a team of Italian archaeologists led by Prof. Emmanuel Anati discovered what appeared to be Paleolithic cave art in Għar Hasan caves. Anati took photos of the team's finds and donated them to the Archaeology Museum in Valletta. Unfortunately, the paintings themselves have since been defaced by modern graffiti and geological erosion. This has given rise to a conspiracy theory that the evidence was obliterated because it conflicted with the much more recent time-frame for human occupation of Malta. Access to the interior of Għar Hasan is no longer possible.

Anati also identified Paleolithic tectiform (roof-shaped) cave art at Għar Dalam and urged further investigation of several caves, which he was willing to undertake at his own expense, but government permission was denied.[13] [Note: some on-line articles describe Anati's Għar Hasan rock-art discoveries as having been at Għar Dalam. This only adds to the confusion.]

Another potential example of Paleolithic art—a bull painted with black manganese oxide—was recorded in the Hal Salfieni Hypogeum (see p. 72) in the 1950s. This raises the possibility that the Hypogeum was a natural cave that was used by people during the Ice Age and was enlarged at a later date (which we know it was) by subsequent inhabitants of Malta. Apparently, paint samples were taken that would have confirmed the painting's pre-Neolithic and probably Paleolithic time frame—but we are unable to find a report describing the results.

The painting is mentioned in David Trump's 1972 book, *Malta—An Archaeological Guide*. However, the painting (if it was a painting) later disappeared and was not mentioned in his later publications.

There are other finds on Malta that have been discredited or ignored, perhaps because they were not found in datable, stratigraphic layers. These include what might be Paleolithic microlithic flints; a Neanderthal-style hand axe; and very old obsidian flakes. Other examples include cart-ruts (see p. 132) that are currently submerged and possible underwater megalithic constructions. These would have had to be constructed when the water level was much lower.[14] This could have been before the end of the last Ice Age, before at least 8,000–10,000 years ago—or more recently, since water levels have continued to rise.

Everybody Has an Agenda

Why would there be (if there is) an effort to discount earlier dates for human habitation on Malta? Is it really because none of these finds are scientifically valid or verifiable? Or is there another reason? Remember, we said earlier that "everybody has an agenda."

Several Maltese researchers, including Anton Mifsud et al., have protested against what they perceived as the biased approach to Maltese prehistory. Francis Aloisio put it this way: "All excavations and research were basically done by our foreign masters, being German, French, Italian, and English. We had one or two Maltese, like Sir Temi Zammit, but ... he was also dismissed. Then, there was the political influence of the time (between the Great Wars) in all this work. The views and research of Ugolini, an Italian, were dismissed because of his 'Fascist' connections."[15]

In *Sirius—the Star of the Maltese Temples*,[16] Lenie Reedijk suggests that the archaeological insistence on a fairly recent date for human habitation on Malta can be traced back to Sir Arthur Evans, an influential, Cambridge-trained, British archaeologist in the early 1900s. He asserted that the first important European civilization—the "cradle" of Western Civilization—had to be Crete. Perhaps not coincidentally, he had just purchased the area around Knossos and was beginning his own archaeological dig there. Hence, megalithic constructions on Malta, a clear sign of a sophisticated culture, could not possibly be older than those on Crete. In addition, similarities between Maltese and Cretan decorative motifs, such as spirals, were considered proof that Malta had borrowed them from Crete.

When improved dating techniques demonstrated the greater age of Malta's temples, the subsequent strategy was to consider Malta an isolated "one-off" example rather than an ancient culture that could have been a source of inspiration to others, including Crete. According to Reedijk, a number of Malta's archaeologists trained under this British archaeologist and his proteges, and they "imbibed" this world view and perpetuated it. Whether that remains a factor today, or whether the evidence is simply too unreliable, we (Elyn and Gary) are in no position to judge.

It is impossible to summarize Reedijk's or Mifsud's arguments here, but they provide fascinating windows into the complex social, political, academic, nationalist, and cultural pressures that continue to influence the archaeological interpretation of Malta. It's a story that includes misrepresentation, theft, and conspiracies—some of which have been described or alluded to in the section above.

The Temples

Malta and Gozo are small islands—Malta is only 17 miles long and 9 miles wide, and Gozo is only 8.7 miles long and 4.5 miles wide. You can easily walk the width of either island in less than a day. Yet as many as 66 megalithic temples were built on these islands between 3600–2350 BCE, give or take a few hundred years—or possibly 9000–4000 BCE, according to Lenie Reedijk.[17] Over a dozen of these sacred sites have survived and can still be visited. Some are only a jumbled pile of stones, but others are more intact and remain very powerful. Seven of the temples (including the underground Hal Saflieni Hypogeum) have been designated UNESCO World Heritage Sites.

> The British Egyptologist T. Eric Peet declared, "Small as Malta is it contains some of the grandest and most important [megalithic] structures of this kind ever erected."[18]

Inevitably, we bring our modern assumptions to our interpretations of what these buildings were and how they were used. We label them temples and identify certain horizontal constructions as altars. We could be wrong. We can say, however, without dispute, that these edifices were constructed by intelligent, highly skilled human beings for very specific purposes, and they were very important places for their communities. Much else is debatable—including why they were built and what they mean.

Many of the surviving temples are massive in size—they are truly "megalithic"—as well as unique in interior layout. They are constructed of either one or both types of local limestone. Most of them are approached via a large, curving forecourt. An impressive trilithon (two upright stones and a lintel stone) forms the entrance. The imposing, more-or-less ovoid perimeter walls of the temples enclose an interior space divided into varying numbers of apses on either side of a central corridor or courtyard. Rubble fills the spaces between the external wall and the walls of the inside apses or lobes. Picture a three- or four- or five- or six-leaf clover with a stem, surrounded by a more-or-less oval frame, with rubble filling the gaps. This design is unique to Malta.

Often, two or three temples were built very close to each other. Sometimes one temple was built intruding into another temple or even wedged between two temples. A number of the temples appear to be "twinned" with another that is 1/4–1/3 mile away.

The temples exist within a landscape, both terrestrial and celestial. They were located where they are for one or more reasons, including the availability of building supplies, fresh water, fertile land, the view, orientation to important landscape features such as hills or valleys, access to the sea, and telluric (see glossary) energies such as underground fault lines or water channels. They also seem to be located in relationship to other sacred sites. In some cases, there is intervisibility of one temple with another. Many, though not all, temples are located on the slope of a hill and facing in a southeasterly or southwesterly direction.

Along with the terrestrial setting, another significant factor is celestial orientation: the direction the temple entryway faces. Although early archaeologists discounted the relationship of sacred sites and astronomical events, archaeo-astronomers are increasingly demonstrating that, in fact, many structures around the world (including Stonehenge, Callanish Stone Circle in Scotland, the Great Pyramid of Giza, Angor Wat, and Maltese temples) were indeed constructed to mark astronomical events, including the cyclical movements of the sun, moon, and stars. We have come a long way from when the respected archaeologist John Evans wrote dismissively in 1959, "There is no sign of any special interest [on the part of the Maltese temple builders] in any object that we see in the sky."[19]

What are the astronomical events that are marked by the temples? That is not always so clear. Klaus Albrecht and others have meticulously measured the orientations of the Maltese temples.[20] Albrecht accounts for the majority of these orientations in terms of the annual movement of the sun. Lenie Reedijk uses the same measurements to explain the alignments in terms of the precession (perceived relative movement) of the star Sirius.[21] Sirius rises and sets at a slightly different location on the horizon over the millennia, and Reedijk believes that the numerous Maltese temples were built sequentially in order to align to these slowly shifting points.

The ancient Maltese master builders took great efforts to build the temples in a way that would create a powerful impression, including constructing large forecourts, massive façades, and imposing trilithon doors. Many have extensive benches built into the façade.

They decorated the insides of the temples. They mixed powdered ochre with water to paint swirling designs on specific areas and to color plastered wall surfaces. They made careful, precise carvings on selected stone blocks and screens. They also used repetitive pecked patterns to create visual interest and, perhaps, to shift states of consciousness. The construction, interior design, and decoration of the temples indicate highly sophisticated intention and impressive engineering expertise.

Much else about the temples is disputable, or at least uncertain. For example, a number of the orthostats (see glossary) have holes cut through them. Some of the holes may have been used for tethering animals before ritual sacrifice or during animal blessing or healing ceremonies. Other holes, found in or next to threshold stones, may have been used to receive libations—but maybe they were used during ritual ablutions. A third kind of hole may have been utilized for hanging partitions. And, finally, another kind of hole, an oracle hole, may have been used for a variety of purposes. Some appear to be oriented so that solar (or lunar) light would shine through the hole into interior chambers; others may have been used to communicate, either with sound or with objects, from one sacred space to another.

These are logical ideas, but we really do not know how most (or all) of these holes were used because we have no written records or oral history from that time. Although we can extrapolate from the artifacts found in the temples, we don't know what rituals the ancient Maltese performed.

In the following section, we will describe a number of the surviving temples, including the two subterranean hypogea (see glossary). We will discuss some of the controversies and conflicts as they arise. We will look at these topics in greater depth in "The Temples: More Controversies" section beginning on p. 114.

For more detailed archaeological descriptions and floor-plans, we recommend David H. Trump's *Malta – Prehistory and Temples* (2008) and Anthony Bonanno's *The Archaeology of Malta & Gozo* (2017). (Appendix 2 provides a list of archaeological phases.) If you plan to visit the temples, we suggest purchasing in advance the relevant Malta Insight Heritage Guides. They have detailed, fold-out floorplans that help to clarify the often-complex temple layouts.

Skorba, near Mġarr, Malta — The oldest prehistoric structures on Malta

Skorba is located in the hamlet of Żebbiegħ, on the outskirts of Mġarr (pronounced mm-jarr), in northern Malta, not to be confused with Mġarr on Gozo. It is approximately 0.6 mile from nearby Ta' Ħaġrat Temples. Skorba is listed as a UNESCO World Heritage Site.

Skorba includes both an early settlement and two later temples. There isn't much to see at the site, but it is significant. David H. Trump excavated it in the early 1960s; it was the first of the Maltese temples to be excavated using modern techniques and technology. Skorba began as an open-air village with huts built of mud brick, placed on stone foundations, dating perhaps to 7,000 years ago. The site has given its name to the Red Skorba and Grey Skorba pottery sequences. The habitations discovered predate the Temple Period (4100–2500 BCE) and are thus the oldest prehistoric structures discovered on the island.

During the excavation, archaeologists uncovered the "Red Skorba" shrine rooms, located east of the Skorba Temples. Trump notes that this suggests there were earlier religious structures that were subsequently built over with later religious structures—a practice that is quite common worldwide and at other locations on Malta (see p. 40; p. 174).[22]

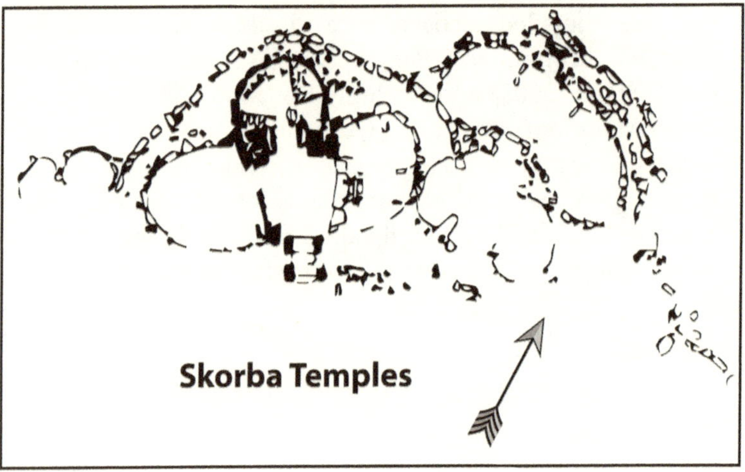

In the shrine rooms, archaeologists discovered a number of broken figures that appear to be female. Five figurines were found in the north room of the shrine; four are terracotta, one stone. Reconstructions from bits and pieces of broken ceramic indicate minimal face sculpting, bosses that represent breasts, exaggerated thighs and buttocks, and an exaggerated pubic triangle. Arms and lower limbs are not represented, nor do the figures appear to wear clothes. A few other broken pieces were discovered at different stratigraphic levels.

Trump judicially says, "Although it has been pointed out that female figurines do not necessarily imply, still less prove, the worship of a Mother Goddess, this remains the most economical explanation of these intriguing objects."[23]

The two Skorba temples are built from hard Coralline Limestone. The older West Temple is from the Ġgantija Phase (beginning around 3600 BCE) and the later East Temple dates to the Tarxien Phase (beginning 3150 BCE). Today, the site is in poor repair. It looks like a bunch of tumbled down stones, although some imposing megaliths are still standing.

The layout of the West Temple was altered and reduced in size over a number of centuries, but it began as a typical Maltese three-apse temple. Some of the stones were covered with pecked, pitted decoration. At the site, the visitor can see the lower level of the foundation, the remains of a wall, paving slabs with "libation holes" in the entrance passage, a doorway to the inner apse, and the *torba* (cement-like) floor. Later Bronze-Age settlers during the Tarxien Cemetery phase (2350–1475 BCE) added internal walls and a bench.

The more recent, East Temple has been even less-well-served by the millennia. Its walls are lower, and it was not even recognized as a temple until late in Trump's excavation. It had a four-apse plan and a shallow niche at the back, and was built onto the side of the older West Temple. Today, this temple is cut through by the footpath outside the enclosure fence.

Entry Information

Tickets are not available at the site. Combined entry tickets to Skorba and nearby Ta' Ħaġrat can be bought online through Heritage Malta, from the Mġarr Snack Bar just off Mġarr's village square, or from the "Farmers Bar" in Zebbiegh (next to Skorba). Check http://heritagemalta.org for details.

Getting There

Skorba is located in the hamlet of Żebbiegħ, on the outskirts of Mġarr, northern Malta. It is approximately 0.6 mile from Ta' Ħaġrat Temples in Mġarr. A regular bus runs from Valletta to Mġarr.

Controversies

Klaus Albrecht's measurements seem to indicate that Skorba West Temple was constructed in alignment with the midwinter sunrise, and Skorba East is aligned to the late morning sun.[24] Lenie Reedijk has a different theory about the alignments of these temples, based on the precession of the star Sirius.[25] Skorba West faced the place on the horizon where Sirius rose in about 5300 BCE, and Skorba East faces toward the hilltop where Sirius rose around 8750 BCE. Note that Reedijk's theory reorganizes the chronology of the temples. The eastern temple would have been built earlier, not later, than the western temple—and presumably, the western temple would then have intruded into the eastern, not vice versa.

Ta' Ħaġrat, Mġarr, Malta — Best-preserved early three-lobe temple

In the center of Mġarr village are the two Ta' Ħaġrat Temples: a main trefoil-shaped (three-lobed) temple to the west and a smaller temple to the east with four, asymmetrical lobed spaces. They are in better repair than the temples at Skorba. As at Skorba, the temples replaced an earlier settlement. Ta' Ħaġrat was designated a UNESCO World Heritage Site because it is "the best-preserved Maltese temple with an early 3-lobe design."

The larger, older "main" or western temple dates from around 3600–3200 BCE and the smaller, more recent one probably dates from 3300–3000 BCE. They are built of hard Coralline

Limestone and are somewhat rough-hewn in comparison with later temples. They are also more irregular and smaller than many other Maltese temples, but they follow a similar pattern of having an ovoid perimeter wall and interior lobes, with rubble filling between.

The somewhat restored trilithon entrance to the western temple remains standing, reached by a set of steps. The impressive doorway is surrounded by a nearly intact façade with a surrounding bench and looming megaliths, making it easy to see the lobed structure. Inside the temple, a central courtyard gives access to three chambers.

The smaller, later, eastern temple on the right penetrates into the first temple. A flight of steps unites the two temples. The smaller temple has four irregular lobes and is built for the most part out of shapeless boulders. Archaeologists disagree about the dating of this temple.[26] One would expect the smaller and cruder temple to have been constructed earlier, but David Trump doesn't think that is the case.

A 1" x 2" limestone model of a simple oval-shaped temple unit was found at Ta' Ħaġrat. This model has revealed a great deal about temple construction. It has a stone roof, indicating that these early temples were roofed, with upper-level corbelling, a trilithon doorway, and alternating "edge-and-side" ("header-and-stretcher") placement of upright wall stones for stability.

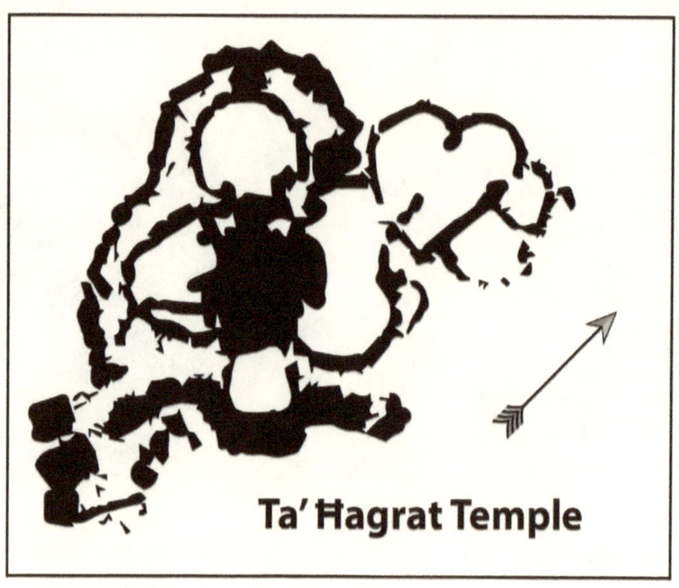

Our Experience at Ta' Ħaġrat

Elyn's Experience: Seen through the surrounding metal fence, the temples looked unkempt and neglected. The guard took our tickets and opened the gate. First, I noticed the large, reconstructed trilithon entrance. Then I noticed the fluttering white butterflies, the buzzing bees, and the almond trees. Francis Aloisio, our private guide, told us that almond trees are "protective," and that's why you find so many around these sacred sites. He also told us that this temple had been "quiet" for millennia but was now awakening and distributing energy around the island.

He said that part of his work is to "intentionally awaken" these ancient Maltese places of power, each of which served (and now serves again) a unique purpose.

I felt an odd kind of sadness and the presence of ancient spirit beings drifting around the stones. I was surprised by how peaceful and calm it was inside the ruined temple, even though outside the enclosure, the wind was whistling. Perhaps the relative stillness was because the temple was situated in a slight depression. Or perhaps it was because it was a powerful place where, if we were attentive, we could still have an encounter with the Sacred.

Gary's Experience: I used my dowsing rods to discover a telluric energy line running at an angle through the main temple toward Mġarr Church. I also located an energy vortex at one of the interior free-standing megaliths, which set my dowsing rod spinning in a circle. None of this was unusual; we usually find vortices and telluric energy lines at sacred sites.

Entry Information

Tickets are not available at the site. Combined entry tickets to Ta' Ħaġrat and Skorba must be bought online from Heritage Malta, from the Mġarr Snack Bar, or from the "Farmers Bar" in Żebbiegħ (next to Skorba). Check http://heritage-malta.org for details.

Getting There

Ta' Ħaġrat Temples are located in Mġarr, northern Malta. A regular bus runs from Valletta to Mġarr.

Controversies

Archaeologists disagree about which Ta' Ħaġrat Temple was built first: David Trump thinks the eastern temple was earliest; Anthony Bonanno thinks the western temple was. According to Lenie Reedijk, Ta' Ħaġrat's main, western temple was oriented to viewing the rising of Sirius circa 4700 BCE, and the smaller, eastern temple was oriented to the rising star in 8800 BCE.[27] This would explain why the eastern temple is smaller and cruder: it is older. However, this would mean that the western temple is intruding into it, rather than the other way around. While Trump might agree with this order of construction, he would not agree with the time frame.

Klaus Albrecht finds a different orientation for the temples.[28] According to him, the main, western temple is aligned with the midwinter sunrise; the smaller temple is aligned almost due south, probably pointing toward what is now Nadur's Tower.

Mġarr Parish Church — Built over a pre-Christian site?

The modern Church of the Assumption in Mġarr, Malta, was constructed in 1946 over an earlier church. It is known as "The Egg Church" because the building was primarily funded by parishioners' sales of eggs, along with poultry and animals.

We have been told that this church was built over the remains of a Neolithic temple. If so, this would not be unusual. Numerous shrines, temples, and churches all over the world have been built over ancient sacred sites, either because it was a way of "cleansing" and "sanctifying" the location or because of a desire to draw on the perceived accumulated spiritual power of the place. We have seen one example of this at Ta' Ħaġrat; we will see other examples associated with holy wells and Marian shrines (see p. 168; p. 179).

Entry Information

Mġarr Parish Church is an active church. Proper attire is required. Check website for schedule. https://www.quddies.com.mt/churches/186/Santa-Marija-Assunta/Mġarr

Getting There

A regular bus runs from Valletta to Mġarr, northern Malta.

Ġgantija Temples, Xagħra, Gozo — A giant must have built them

Ġgantija's two temples are truly massive, giving rise to the legend that they were built by a giantess in a single night while she held her child in one arm (or on her back), carried a stone on her head, and ate beans. Female multi-tasking is obviously not a new concept. Not surprisingly, the name Ġgantija (dje-gant-ee-ya) means giantess.

Ġgantija's temples are the only remaining megalithic temples on Gozo. They date from approximately 3600 BCE for the South Temple and from 3200 BCE for the North Temple. These temples, which are the two largest on Malta and Gozo, are also two of the oldest and are remarkably well preserved. It is interesting to note that they are thought to have been built during the same time period as the much smaller and "cruder" Skorba and Ta' Ħaġrat Temples. And, like those, they are on the UNESCO World Heritage list.

The temples are impressive in size, complexity of layout, and the gargantuan dimensions of some of their limestone blocks. The South and North Temples have separate entrances and curved facades but are enclosed within the same massive perimeter wall. They are oriented toward the southeast, which suggests a Winter Solstice Sunrise alignment.

The perimeter wall currently stands over 20' high, and together the temples span over 131'. One corner of the South Temple stands 23' high. With the addition of horizontal courses of stone, the wall may have originally stood as high as 52'. The remains of upper-level corbelling can still be seen, indicative of some kind of roof structure. Researchers haven't figured out how the megalith builders constructed this wall—or the rest of the temples—without the use of metal tools or wheeled vehicles to transport such huge stones.

The exterior wall that encloses the temples was built of hard Coralline Limestone; the more-easily-worked Globigerina Limestone was used for the inside construction, including room dividers and altar-like stones. The Coralline blocks are local, but the Globigerina had to be dragged uphill from a quarry at a lower elevation ½ mile away.

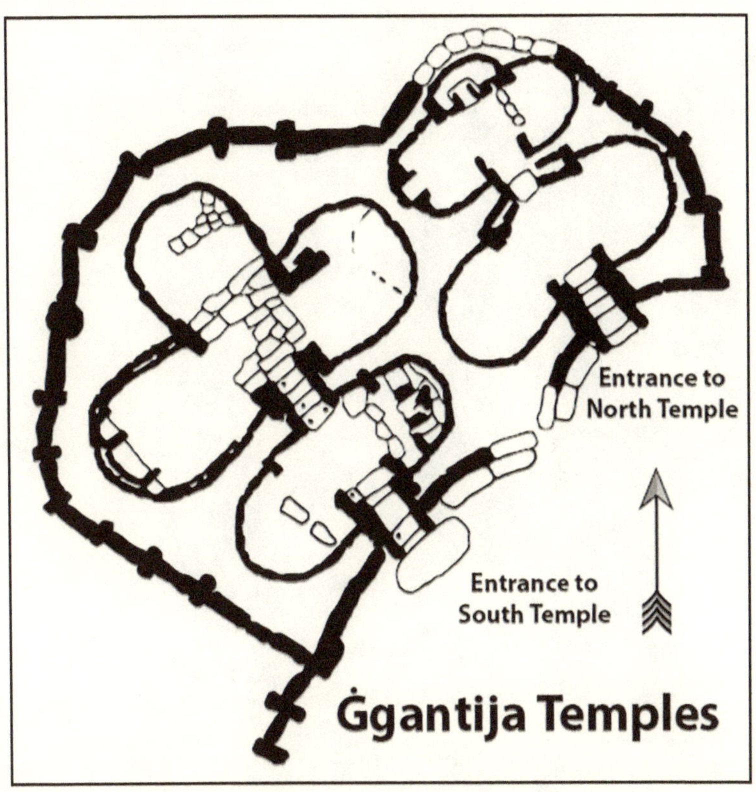

The modern Ġgantija Interpretation Center, located on the south edge of Xagħra (shaa-ra), controls access to the temples. The multi-media exhibits are quite informative and worth examining at length. They include numerous archaeological finds from Xagħra Circle and Hypogeum as well as from Ġgantija.

Access to the temples is through the rear door of the Interpretation Center. The long and winding Heritage Park sidewalk leads past various landscaped areas and instructive plaques describing the local flora, including carob trees and indigenous Aleppo pines, and fauna. The picturesque views of the surrounding countryside are noteworthy.

Slightly below the crest of the hill, the back of the massive grey Coralline Limestone perimeter wall comes into view. Using a masonry technique known as "header-and-stretcher" (or "edge-and-side"), huge flat upright stones were alternately placed face-out and end-out, thus enhancing the stability of the wall. The Heritage Park sidewalk leads around to the expansive courtyard in front of the curving twin entrances. This courtyard was artificially terraced to create a large, flat place for (we presume) community gatherings.

Before entering, it is worth turning around and looking at the landscape. Ġgantija lies on the edge of the Xagħra central plateau, with a view to the southern part of Gozo. Irrigated fields, some of them terraced, soften the terrain. Hills, scattered settlements, and a church are visible in the distance. Although the settlement patterns are different today from 5,500 years ago, the geography is very similar.

The older, South Temple is on the left; the North Temple is on the right. Thousands of years after it was constructed, after millennia of exposure to rain and wind, the South Temple's façade still soars to a height of more than 23'. The extensive and unsightly metal scaffolding is designed to keep the massive upright stones from shifting and the walls from collapsing. Raised walkways with metal railings lead through the large orthostats into the temples.

The South Temple has five apses/lobes, arranged off a central corridor. Although the railings on either side of the walkways keep the visitor from entering most of the side chambers, there is still much to explore and to experience.

The threshold slab in the South Temple has four holes on each side, perhaps for libations or ritual ablutions. A 4'-high snake carved in relief once climbed up a Globigerina Limestone upright slab in an alcove in this temple, but it now resides in the Ġgantija Interpretation Center. Spiral relief patterns are still visible on some of the stones on the altar-like construction in the first alcove on the right, along with faint residues of reddish ochre still visible if the light is right. We say "altar-like" because it looks like an altar, but we don't actually know how it was used.

As one walks through the South Temple, one notices various holes in upright stones, decorative engravings (spirals, pitted relief designs, etc.), and different altar-like constructions. At the rear of the temple are several constructions worth spending time with. In the left-hand alcove is a trilithon altar composed of three table-like constructions side to side. In the right-hand alcove is a circular hearth stone and a bench altar.

The rough appearance of the walls is misleading. Originally, the Coralline blocks were covered with plaster and painted in red ochre. They would have presented a much smoother and finer appearance.

The North Temple, which is slightly smaller and less decorated, was built after the South Temple, probably around 3200–3100 BCE. At that time, part of the South Temple's north perimeter wall was removed. This allowed the North Temple to be built next to the South Temple. The perimeter wall was then reconstructed to enclose the North Temple as well, so that both are contained within the same enclosure.

The North Temple has a four-lobe layout: the terminal fifth lobe of the South Temple has been replaced by a shallow niche. Its building style is also different. Most stones are left in an "undressed" state, rather than being as carefully finished as in the South Temple.

Our Experience at Ġgantija

Elyn's Experience: It's difficult for me to talk about what happened to me in Ġgantija Temple a number of years ago. I had wandered off from the small, sacred sites tour I was on and ended up alone, facing the stone altar in the terminal apse of Ġgantija South. For some reason, I felt the urge to raise my arms in a gesture of invocation. Suddenly, a group of translucent priests in full-length white robes and white headgear "appeared" behind the altar. I was so startled I didn't know what to do except turn around and run.

When I returned to Ġgantija Temple the following year, I was better prepared. In fact, I was hoping I would meet the priests again. I walked slowly toward the back of the temple and waited until I was alone. I raised my arms in invocation—and there they were again. This time, instead of running away, I asked them questions. Our communication wasn't through spoken word, and most of it is too personal to disclose. This much I can reveal, however. They told me: It isn't about "sharing the stories"—it's about sending blessings from the heart. Over the years, the meaning of that cryptic communication has unfolded for me and I have tried to put it into action. Instead of being angry, send blessings. Instead of being frustrated or disappointed, send blessings. Instead of feeling helpless—send blessings.

Entry Information

Entrance is included in Heritage Malta Multisite Pass. See http://heritagemalta.org.

Getting There

Ġgantija Temples are located in Xagħra, central Gozo, accessible from the island of Malta via ferry. Regular Gozo buses run between Victoria, Marsalforn, Ramla Bay, Mġarr (Gozo) and Xagħra. Both "Hop On Hop Off" bus services stop at Ġgantija. Taxi service is also available. Xagħra is a village with various restaurants and other attractions.

Controversies

According to Klaus Albrecht and other researchers, Ġgantija Temples are aligned to the (southeast) sunrise of the winter solstice.[29] The sun rises behind the modern Nadur church, which is located at the highest point on the horizon. Lenie Reedijk has a different interpretation.[30] Because of the orientations of the entryways, it is her belief that Ġgantija North is the earlier temple and dates to the rising of Sirius in 5350 BCE; Ġgantija South dates to the rising of Sirius in 4250 BCE. This would explain why the North Temple is smaller, simpler, and slightly cruder: it's older. We don't know if it would explain the way in which the perimeter wall was expanded. As always, note that Reedijk's theory results in a very different chronology from the archaeological consensus.

Xagħra Circle/Hypogeum, Xagħra, Gozo — An underground mortuary temple and cemetery

Ġgantija Temples and Xagħra Circle/Hypogeum are both located within the small town of Xagħra (shaa-ra) and are only separated by 1/4 mile. Xagħra Circle is west of Ġgantija. Both the temples and the hypogeum were in active use during some of the same centuries, so we infer there was some connection between them, although we don't know exactly what that was.

Xagħra Circle/Hypogeum is an underground funerary temple and burial site constructed by expanding a subterranean system of natural caves. Xagħra Circle has recently been renamed Xagħra Hypogeum, which is Greek for "underground chamber." This is a more accurate description of the site, which was originally surrounded by a circular wall of Coralline Limestone megaliths, now gone. The Circle/Hypogeum opened to the east, facing in the direction of Ġgantija Temples.

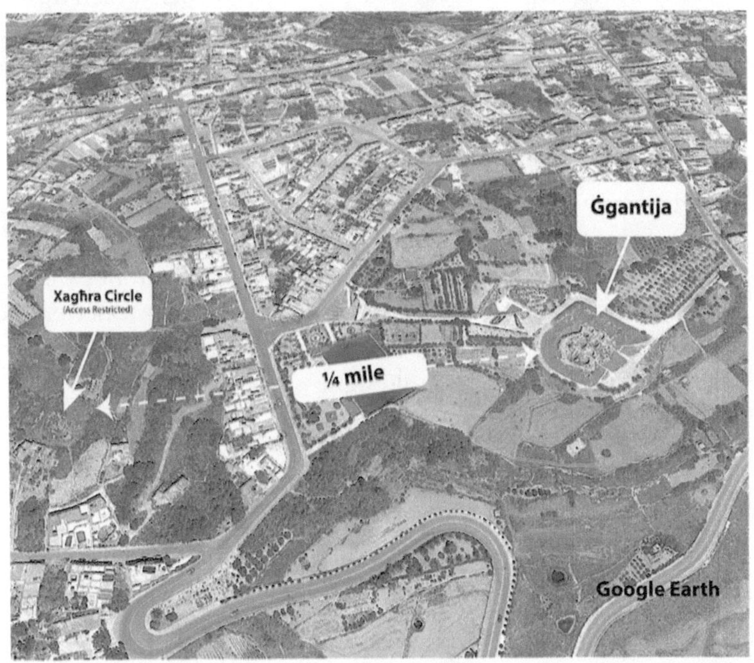

Although it is not unusual to bury people underground, having an underground mortuary building is quite uncommon. However, there are several others on Malta, including the impressive Ħal Saflieni Hypogeum, which is a very popular tourist site (see p. 58). Unlike Ħal Saflieni Hypogeum, the only way to visit Xagħra Hypogeum is to pay for a private tour with a Heritage Malta guide.

Both Hypogea appear to be paired with nearby megalithic temples: Xagħra Hypogeum is paired with Ġgantija Temples, and Ħal Saflieni Hypogeum is paired with Tarxien Temples. Archaeologists have not yet determined whether Ħal Saflieni Hypogeum or Xagħra Hypogeum is older.

Xagħra Circle/Hypogeum has been explored by an Anglo-Maltese team of archaeologists off and on since 1987. The site was initially excavated (or more correctly, torn up) by the British Governor of Gozo, Lieutenant John Otto Bayer, in the 1820s. No records of Bayer's excavation have been found, but, fortunately, his activities were recorded by C. F. de Brocktorff in detailed watercolor drawings. Farmers later reclaimed their land, which had been confiscated by Bayer for his excavations, and by the 1840s they had intentionally buried the site under vineyards. Over time, the location of the site was lost, and almost all of the standing stones that formed the Coralline Limestone circular boundary wall were carted away for reuse. You can see at least one incorporated into the side of a nearby building.

In the 1960s, the enterprising Gozitan policeman and amateur historian Joseph Attard Tabone used clues in Brocktorff's drawings and other early reports to track down the likely location of the lost circle. His efforts saved the site from subsequent development and destruction: the government had planned to put a road through it.

David Trump described the deceptively unimpressive site as it appeared in 1972: "In the fields west again [from Ġgantija] are traces of what appears to have been a very important site. Colt Hoare noticed it in 1790. Brocktorff in 1827 painted a large stone circle here, with attached structures, but a few blocks of stone built into field walls and a thin scatter of sherds among the crops are all that one can find today."[31]

About 15 years later, an Anglo-Maltese research group began conducting modern, scientific excavations in Xagħra Circle. Excavating Xagħra Circle is a dangerous activity because of the particularly friable (crumbly) nature of the limestone in this area. The initial work lasted from 1987–1994; after a pause, this group, now based at Queen's University of Belfast under the leadership of Prof. Caroline Malone, has continued to excavate to the present day. Their research is changing what is known about Malta's (or at least Gozo's) prehistory.

Material recovered from the Xagħra Circle, including human remains and pottery sherds, has been dated from approximately 4100–2700 BCE. It is important to realize that the mortuary temple itself was not constructed nor in use throughout that entire period, and that the Xagħra Circle location was in use long before the nearby Ġgantija Temples were built.

The earliest utilization of the area dates to between 4100–3700 BCE. Archaeologists have discovered the remains of a village and a well-preserved, two-chambered, rock-cut tomb reached by a shaft.

Later, the collective/communal subterranean cemetery known as the Xagħra Hypogeum was developed. A paved path led from a huge trilithon (its remains are now hidden by an immense cactus) to a set of steps that descended into the large underground limestone cavern. The cavern was created by expanding an existing underground network of caves. A statue-menhir (an upright stone with a human face) was found near the entrance. Ceremonies appear to have been held in a central shrine area, where altar-like stones with pitted decoration and remains of ochre, stone "screens," and ritual deposits have been found. A large stone jar, possibly for libations, was also found in the central area.

Understanding this powerful place and its shifting usage over time has been made difficult because, at some point during its history, the limestone roof covering the central cavern collapsed. Skeletal remains have been found both below and above the resulting rubble, indicating that the site continued to be used as a mortuary.

According to Albert, our Heritage Malta guide, the subterranean space was probably a collective ossuary for secondary burial. A number of excavated bones had been covered with ochre—which could only happen after they no longer had flesh on them. In other words, the decaying bodies were buried (or left out in the open); subsequently, the bones were recovered, sprinkled with ochre, separated by type, and re-buried inside Xagħra Circle. It appears that social hierarchy was unimportant—or at least had no bearing after death—since there was no ongoing separation of individuals "laid to rest" with specific grave goods for eternity.

However, there were also completely articulated skeletons found on the floor of the cave and in special pits. This suggests that either earlier burial practices included individual entombment or that those individuals were considered special.

Approximately 220,000 bones have been recovered, belonging more or less equally to men and women, with a predominance of pre-adults. This is the equivalent of between 500–800 individuals. 450 offering bowls have been discovered, each of which might represent an individual deceased. Since many more people lived (and hence died) on Gozo during the time span in which the Hypogeum was in use, there must be other burials or cemetery locations that have not yet been discovered.

A number of impressive grave goods have been discovered, including ceramics, over 700 beads, V-perforated buttons, miniature axes, and obese statuettes. The exceedingly amply proportioned statuettes (huge buttocks and legs, very heavy arms, usually flat upper torsos, tiny feet) are quite unusual and relevant to the question of Mother Goddess worship on Malta. They are usually called "Fat Lady" statuettes, but for reasons that will become clear (see p. 124), we refer to them as obese statuettes.

Twin "obese people" statuette from
Xaghra Circle/Hypogeum
(Ggantija Interpretation Center)

One small limestone carving shows two obese people (one headless), wearing pleated skirts, sitting on an elaborately detailed bed or couch. The statuette is 3.5" deep x 5" wide x 5.5" high. The gender of the two people is not clearly specified, but they have ample proportions, including very plump arms, enormous legs, and tiny feet that peek out from under their pleated skirts. One holds a miniature person on its lap; the other holds a cup or bowl. They don't have noticeable breasts but, instead, heavily padded chests. The statuette was originally painted red, black, and yellow. Traces of red ochre can still be seen on the legs and parts of the couch.

A dozen or so extremely corpulent clay figurines, about 3" high, were also found at Xaghra. They appear to be sitting on their enormous buttocks. They have small heads, some of which are tilted back; huge thighs and big calves; ample arms; very flat upper torsos—and no indications of clothing. They appear to be holding a round disk against their chests, but it might be an indication of something else. David Trump says two of these figurines have breasts.[32] A 3' high, limestone obese figure once stood somewhere in the hypogeum, but it was later shattered (perhaps ritually destroyed?) and its pieces scattered throughout the area.

Nine enigmatic Globigerina Limestone figures, erroneously referred to as "the shaman's cache," were found packed together, as if they had been stored inside a perishable container (a leather pouch, perhaps). Six of them are highly stylized; their carved human heads are perched on top of flat, wedge-shaped bodies without arms or legs. They are 7.5" x 2". Each figurine could have been grasped in one hand, inserted into soft earth or sand, or perhaps slipped under a belt. They are totally unlike the corpulent statuettes. The six stylized figurines appear to be in different stages of completion, though it's possible that this is an intentional progression. Two have detailed heads and carved indications of a belt and lower-body clothing. One is a roughed-out "blank," another has a face that is ½ carved, ½ unfinished.

The other three figurines in "the shaman's cache" are much shorter and also unique. One resembles a pig's head on a short stick; one is a human head on a short column with a splayed base; and one appears to be a human head perched on an arched, bent tube, possibly representing a very stylized body (front legs, rear hindquarters).

Perhaps this "cache" contained works-in-progress deposited as personal grave goods with the suddenly deceased sculptor. Or perhaps they were used in ceremony to represent the incompleteness of life, or of life coming into form from formlessness—or life returning from form to formlessness. Perhaps they were visual aids for storytelling in a ritual setting. Or perhaps they were a deposit of partly completed objects for some other reason.

Among other items found in the central area is a set of six or eight tiny carved cow carpal-bone figures with human heads, each one measuring about 1" x 0.2". Because the bone material was soft, it was easy to carve.

Our Experience at Xagħra Circle

Elyn's Experience: We pushed our way through the lush undergrowth, avoiding as much as possible the profusion of waist-high spiky plants, admiring the bright red poppies and exuberantly golden flowers in full bloom, the butterflies dancing and the bees humming. Albert, our guide, blazed the way. Soon we reached the metal fence that surrounds Xagħra Circle. He unlocked the gate and we walked up to the edge of a large open cavity. "Be careful!" he said, pointing to a hole in the ground near our feet, almost hidden in weeds. "That's a pit." He pointed out where different parts of the hypogeum had been discovered, uncovered, and covered up again by archaeologists to protect the site.

It's true that there isn't much to see—but there was a lot to feel as the wind ruffled my hair and the air filled with the scent of flowers. I circumnavigated the subterranean mortuary site, being careful not to walk too close to the edge or step into a vine-covered hole. Even after all these millennia, the energy was still palpable. I could tell that I was walking on sacred ground.

Entry Information

Xagħra Circle/Hypogeum is not accessible without prior appointment. The site is surrounded by a high boundary fence. On the one hand, there is not much to see since the large hollow central cavity is filled in with sandbags and plastic tarpaulins. On the other hand, it is a rare opportunity to visit a major site without being surrounded by hordes of tourists. You can make an appointment online with Heritage Malta and pay for access and/or for a private tour (http:// heritagemalta.org/contact-us/). It is worth paying the small additional fee for the guided tour; our guide was extremely knowledgeable.

Getting There

Regular Gozo buses run between Victoria, Marsalforn, Ramla Bay, Mġarr, and Xagħra. Xagħra Circle is in the village of Xagħra in central Gozo. Both "Hop On Hop Off" bus services stop at Ġgantija Temples, where you will probably go to meet your guide. Taxi service is also available. Xagħra is a village with various restaurants and other attractions.

Controversies

Based on their research at Xagħra Circle/Hypogeum, Prof. Malone and her team are rewriting the timeline of Neolithic settlement on Malta. So far, they have moved the earliest date back to 5900 BCE and determined that there were two waves of ancient settlers. The first group arrived around 5900 BCE and left around 4800 BCE. The second group arrived around 3850 BCE—and a mere 200 years later began building, without precedent, the massive, unique megalithic temples.

Most archaeological timelines date Xagħra and several sites on Malta to 4100 BCE. That date, according to Prof. Caroline Malone, is after the first group of settlers left and before the second group arrived—so there shouldn't have been anybody there. Perhaps Malone's findings describe the situation at Xagħra Circle/Hypogeum on Gozo but not on Malta? Or does the 4100 BCE date need to be revised for Malta as well? Or, perhaps, the first group of settlers never left but instead diminished greatly in numbers or stopped using the site for 1000 years. We describe some of Malone's findings on p. 12.

Ħal Saflieni Hypogeum, Paola, Malta — A multi-level, subterranean temple and mortuary site

Ħal Saflieni Hypogeum (hul saf-lee-ni) is an awe-inspiring underground site excavated out of the underlying Globigerina Limestone. The site was in use from 4000–2500 BCE, during which time the three-level subterranean cemetery/mortuary temple was dug in stages. This time frame overlaps with when Xagħra Circle/Hypogeum on Gozo was in active use. Like Xagħra Hypogeum, Ħal Saflieni Hypogeum is ¼ mile to the west of its paired temple site—in this case, Tarxien Temples. This unique construction is a UNESCO World Heritage Site.

The Hypogeum was discovered by accident and quickly concealed. Sometime between 1900–1902, construction workers broke into the top of the Hypogeum while putting in foundations and digging wells for an urban development. Rather than tell anyone official, they continued their building project. Only when they were finished were the authorities informed.

Archaeological excavations were begun in 1903 by Father Emanuel Magri, SJ (Society of Jesus). He only had access to the middle and lower levels because access to the upper level was still in private hands. He extracted large quantities of fragmented bones apparently embedded at random in red dirt. Much of the material finds, especially the numerous skeletal remains, were discarded as being of limited scientific value—which they were, at that time.

One government document indicates Fr. Magri had completed his work in 1906, at which time he was suddenly called away for missionary work to Sfax, Tunisia. He unexpectedly died there in 1907, without publishing a report of his findings. However, a recently discovered letter describes his investigations in some detail. He stated that finds, such as bones and broken terracotta, had been thrown in sans ordre (without any order). The bones were very fragmented, and only a few skulls could be saved. According to his letter, what he found was a complete jumble of earth, human, and cultural material.

British Egyptologist T. Eric Peet wrote the following in 1912: "When the museum authorities took over the Hypogeum practically all the chambers were filled to within a short distance of the roofs with a mass of reddish soil, which proved to contain the remains of thousands of human skeletons. In other words, Ħal Saflieni was used as a burial place, though this may not have been its original purpose [italics added]. The bones lay for the most part in disorder, and so thickly that in the space of about 4 cubic yards lay the remains of no less than 120 individuals. One skeleton, however, was found intact, lying on the right side in the crouched position, i.e. with arms and knees bent up...The bodies themselves were so damaged with damp that only ten skulls could be saved whole."[33]

Model of the Hal Saflieni Hypogeum in the National Museum of Archaeology

Sir Themistocles Zammit, the "father of Maltese archaeology," took up the excavation but without the benefit of Magri's lost records. Between 1907–1911 he salvaged what he could and expanded the dig. Apparently, the bones he found were also heaped together in a haphazard manner. Zammit suggested that this could be part of a Neolithic burial practice of secondary burial, during which the soft tissue was removed and then the bones deposited together. In other words, the Hypogeum might have been an ossuary—just like Xagħra Circle/Hypogeum or the Catacombs of Paris.

Zammit roughly extrapolated that the skeletal remains of approximately 7,000 people were discovered in the initial dig, buried in earth throughout the lower levels of the Hypogeum. Along with numerous bones, a beautiful plate decorated with incised bulls and goats was also found. Other artifacts include the famous tiny terracotta "Sleeping Lady" and two small, reclining-on-couch figurines; other statuettes, including 2.5" high alabaster obese statuettes with their right hands extended downward and their left hands crossed over their waists; a 15" x 10.5" headless statue with two "exchangeable" limestone heads found beside it; beads; amulets in the form of miniature polished stone axes; and carved animals and birds. Some of these may have been grave goods; others may have been ritual deposits or items used in ceremony.

Ħal Saflieni Hypogeum's sprawling, labyrinthian floorplan covers approximately 5,382 sq. feet and comprises three levels, which go down to a depth of 46' below street level. It includes 30+ rooms, niches, alcoves, halls, steps—including the "Holy of Holies," an impressive room that resembles an above-ground sanctuary, complete with carved trilithons and a corbelled roof. Because the lower levels of the Hypogeum were undamaged by weathering, human intrusion, or subsequent building projects, they have provided an unparalleled opportunity for researchers to understand how above-ground temples were constructed and decorated.

The main axis runs NW–SE and is oriented in the direction of the winter-solstice sunrise, an appropriate orientation for a mortuary temple since the winter solstice marks the longest night and shortest day, and the beginning of the return of light. We can only imagine what ceremonies of celebration would have taken place deep within the Hypogeum, lit by light coming down from above.[34]

The Hypogeum looks a bit like a frosted Swiss-cheese cake of three unequal layers constructed from the top down. The top or Upper Level is the oldest, dating from sometime between 3600–3000 BCE. The Middle and Lower Layers date from 3000–2500 BCE, with the lowest level being the most recent. We will explore them one by one.

Today the Hypogeum is hidden within a large visitor's center surrounded by houses. Initially, it looked quite different. Excavations of the original ground level have revealed pottery sherds dating back to 4000 BCE. At some point, the land was leveled off and an above-ground megalithic structure was built.

The first underground level of the Hypogeum was created by expanding a natural cave or caves. This Upper Level was carved out of living Globigerina Limestone sometime between 3600–3000 BCE, during what is known archaeologically as the Ġgantija Phase. Although this Upper Level is below ground level, it was partly open to the sky, enabling light to enter into the Hypogeum.

Some of the structures in the Upper Level were not destroyed by later building projects. These include a trilithon archway of two large upright stones and a lintel. Anthony Pace thinks that visitors to the Hypogeum would have had to walk over two tombs in the floor—perhaps a rite of passage—before entering a lobby-like space that had a number of low chambers or niches cut into the side walls.[35] Many of these niches have sunken floors or hollows, which may have contained earth and been used as repositories for burials.

In other words, visitors would be walking through a sacred site that served, at least in part, as a mausoleum. We can imagine that this might have been similar to modern visitors walking through Westminster Abbey, where more than 3,300 people are buried. They, too, walk over tombs embedded in the floor, and there are numerous other tombs in niches along the walls and in individual chapels. Westminster Abbey is a mausoleum—but it is much more than that. And so, too, was the Hypogeum.

The ancient builders also excavated a stone cistern at the Upper Level, apparently to provide the site with water. It remained in use long after the Hypogeum was sealed off.

The Middle Level is accessed through a transitional passage leading to what Pace describes as an internal lobby that also functioned as a light channel. This level is the one that contains a number of impressive, decorated chambers. At least one chamber has a sunken floor, and soil marks indicate that it may once have been filled with earth. Soil marks are also visible on several other walls, including in the Main Chamber.

The "Holy of Holies" room is found in the innermost part of the Middle Level. It was modeled after and resembles aboveground temples. It is curved in shape and is decorated with trilithon arches, niches carved into stone, and a corbelled ceiling. The vertical pillars have pitted decorations similar to that found in a number of above-ground temples. The detailed interior design of the "Holy of Holies" has helped researchers reconstruct how the above-ground temple sanctuaries would have looked.

Carefully designed openings in walls and placement of chambers permitted direct light and indirect light to penetrate into the Middle Level rooms. Morning sunlight would have filtered down and illuminated the façade of the "Holy of Holies" on the winter solstice. One can imagine people moving from light into shadow, from illumination into darkness and back again, as they journeyed deeper into the Hypogeum. How much light depended on many factors, including the changing angle of the sun throughout the year.

The Main Chamber includes a series of recesses carved into the circular walls on two levels, as well as pitted decoration on several of the pillars. Perhaps the recesses were niches that held statues—or perhaps they held the dead. The "Holy of Holies" is intervisible with this chamber; in fact, it was originally accessed through a raised doorway in the Main Chamber.

Another important room in the Middle Level is the so-called Oracle Room. When one tones a particular low frequency (110–111 Hertz, about A at the bottom of the bass staff) into a high niche in the wall, the room resonates. This vibration reverberates throughout the room and carries into the adjoining spaces. Modern research has shown that this frequency has specific physical and mental effects. Whether this is intentional has been subject to debate.

Intricate swirling designs in red ochre decorate the ceiling in the Oracle Room as well as the wall and roof of the Decorated Room. Some of these designs resemble spirals and interlocking bee-hive-like hexagons; some are twisting tendrils that recall a stylized Tree of Life. A faint but still visible checkered pattern of black-and-white squares adorns a section of the wall of the Main Chamber.

An intriguing pit, nearly 6' deep and bell-shaped, is located in an enclosed recess next to the Main Chamber and the stairs leading to the Lower Level. There are openings in the surrounding wall and a ledge around the well-finished pit. The exquisite terracotta "Sleeping Lady" statuette was found here. Archaeologists have suggested that the pit might have been used for ritual deposits or for keeping snakes, hence its name "The Snake Pit."

The "Sleeping Lady" is 5" x 3". She is a typically corpulent Maltese statuette, of ample proportions—except she has large breasts—and wearing what appears to be a skirt. She is lying on her right side on a couch, her tiny head resting on a cushion. She is asleep, in a trance, or dreaming. Some writers suggest she represents death, but it seems more likely, given her appearance, that her somnolent state is indicative of the ancient practice of dream incubation. During this ritual practice (well documented, for example, in Classical Greece at the temple of the healing god Asclepios at Epidaurus), a person would undergo careful preparation before sleeping in a sacred place with the intention of seeking a dream for healing or for information. What better place for such an experience than in the Hypogeum! [Note: This is the same position—reclining, on the right side, used in modern Daoist dream practices.]

The Lower Level is reached through a trilithon and via "the Seven Uneven Steps." It has numerous small niches and a complicated design. Its five main chambers are separated by walls about 6' high. Some of the lower cavities appear to be tunnels leading to—exactly what, is unknown. Lois Jessop reportedly crawled through one of these in the 1930s (see p. 76). Perhaps the rooms were used for storage. Traces of red ochre can be seen on many of the walls, which suggests that whatever this level was used for, it was related to the sacred.

Access is currently restricted, and the guided tour does not go into the Lower Level.

This brief tour of the Hypogeum has described only some of the numerous chambers, rooms, pits, and niches, but they are the highlights as we understand them today. How was this complex space used? We can only speculate, based on partial information and our modern preconceptions.

There is no doubt that the Hypogeum is a place where the living and (at least some of) the dead co-existed, where consciousness was altered through sensory manipulation—shifting and flickering light, darkness, echoing sounds, perhaps fragrances.... Was it primarily a mortuary temple? A place of dreaming and initiation? A place to celebrate the Winter Solstice? Probably all of this—and much more than we can know.

Our Experience in the Hypogeum

Elyn's Experience: Every time I go into the Hypogeum I become disoriented and confused, even though the modern walkway we follow has sturdy metal handrails and is well lighted. With each step that takes me deeper underground, I become more overwhelmed with sensory stimulation—an odd thing in such a quiet and darkened place. But so it is. I have no doubt (though I recognize that, of course, there is plenty of room to doubt) that initiation rituals and dream incubation were conducted in the Middle Level. One only has to look to ancient Mystery Schools for similarities.

I believe that sensory deprivation and sensory stimulation were important aspects of the process. Here, lying on a cot in an enclosed space in semi-darkness, with one's right ear pressed down to listen to the wisdom of the Earth ... perhaps with flickering lamplight revealing swirling patterns in the ceiling above, patterns that seemed to come alive and dance and move of their own volition, perhaps with reverberating tones echoing from a nearby room—here, buried within the Earth, one could enter into a deep trance state. Perhaps the purpose was inner transformation; perhaps it was to encounter the Underworld deities or one's ancestors; perhaps it was to have a dream of healing; perhaps it was a multi-media initiatory process. Here, in the Middle Level of the Hypogeum, surrounded by the remains of the dead, one could enter deeply into the Otherworld, the Afterworld, the Other Realms. Here, one could have a transformational encounter.

Gary's Experience: I am a retired university music professor and adept at finding the resonant frequency of an enclosed space. I quickly found the correct pitch of the Oracle Room and began sounding it. Instantly, the tone was amplified and the space began to vibrate. As the sound bounced back and forth, it created an echo that seemed to come from everywhere and nowhere at the same time. Within moments, our state of consciousness began to alter. Our Heritage Malta guide smiled knowingly. It has been scientifically proven that certain frequencies can shift brain waves from an active to a more meditative state. The ancient master builders knew this long before modern technological devices discovered it.

Entry Information

Tours take place on the hour and are limited to 70 people per day, admitted in groups of 10. It is very important to book your ticket online, often months in advance, at http://heritagemalta.org.

Sometimes it is possible to purchase a last-minute ticket the day before, for the noon and 4 pm tours, at the ticket desks of Fort St. Elmo, Valletta, Malta, and the Gozo Archaeological Museum. But don't count on it.

The 50-minute tour begins with a recently revised multi-media presentation in a room in the visitors' center. The subterranean guided visit includes an individual hand-held audio-guide and takes about 20 minutes. Staff-members accompany the tour groups and occasionally share interesting information.

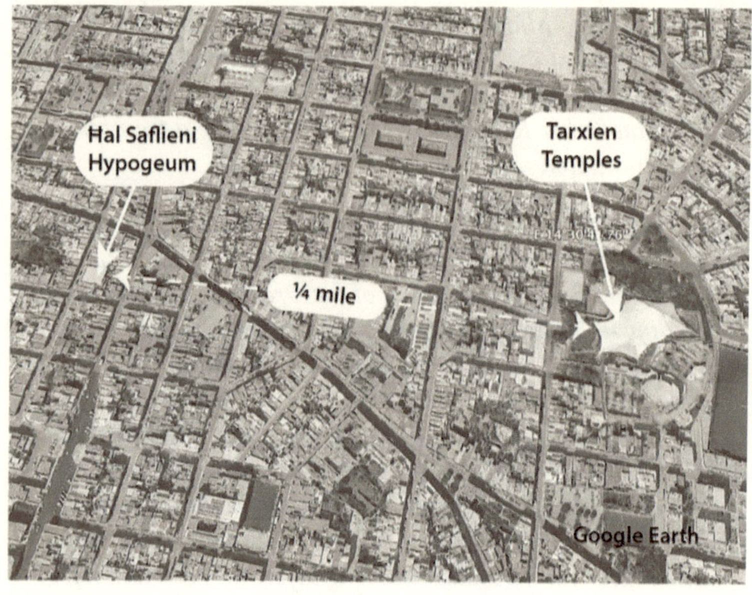

Getting There

The Hypogeum is located in Paola, central Malta, fairly close to Valletta and to the airport. Regular buses stop in the main square in Paola; the Hypogeum is about a five-minute walk from the bus stop. Walk down Triq Hal Luqa to Triq Ic-Cimiterju and turn right. Malta Sightseeing Hop-On-Hop Off South/Red tour has a stop for Tarxien Temples and the Hypogeum. Tarxien Temples, with which the Hypogeum is "paired," are about a 15-minute walk from the Hypogeum or 10 minutes from the main square in Paola.

Controversies

Numerous controversies and conspiracies surround this evocative powerful place.

First: How were the bodies deposited in the Hypogeum?

Was it really filled with dirt and decaying bodies, a singularly unhygienic practice? Fr. Magri, who conducted the first dig, described finding a helter-skelter assortment of crumbling bones buried in large quantities of red earth.

We have read several accounts that suggest that, when one level of the Hypogeum filled up with earth and decaying bodies, another level was excavated below, digging through the dirt and decay. This image is breath-takingly lurid and rather nonsensical. Why excavate such a beautiful underground temple in the Middle Level if it's only going to be filled with decaying bodies? Besides, farmers—even 5,000 years ago—would have been aware of the health danger of being too close to rotting corpses. They didn't need a germ theory to see what happened to dead animals left out in the open. Not to mention the stench.

Sir Themistocles Zammit, who continued the dig after Fr. Magri had died in Tunisia, suggested the Hypogeum may have been an ossuary—a secondary burial site. What supporting evidence can we find for this hypothesis? Archaeologists think that Xagħra Circle Hypogeum on Gozo was in use during the same time span as Ħal Saflieni Hypogeum. Using advanced technology and very careful excavation methods, they have determined that Xagħra served as an ossuary. After the bodies had decayed somewhere else, the bones were carefully sorted into various classifications and piled together. It would make sense that Ħal Saflieni Hypogeum would have been used in the same way. But if so, how can we explain the jumble of earth, grave goods, and crumbling bones discovered in the initial digs?

One "alternative" suggestion is that a powerful flood swept soil and perhaps numerous skeletons from somewhere on higher ground into the most available site: the wide-open entrance to the Hypogeum. That would explain the total disorder and the presence of large quantities of earth. In their discussion of cataclysmic events on Malta, Anton Mifsud et al. state, "It is evident...that the human remains in the underground labyrinth were transmitted there by water action; their matrix of red earth derived from the fields surrounding the monument. In the same manner that the deposits of extinct fauna were laid down in the lower layers of Għar Dalam, the human remains deposited in the Hypogeum have been carried down into the monument from the surface, particularly from the intramural sepulchers (stone-cut tombs) described by Caruana."[36]

We don't know if there is supporting evidence for such a watery cataclysm to have occurred after the Hypogeum was no longer in use. If it did occur, that could explain why its use suddenly ended, and why the temple builders stopped building and left the island around 2500 BCE. Wouldn't you want to leave if one of your most sacred sites had been so completely desecrated—not to mention being afraid of a repeat event?

This cataclysmic event could explain the huge amount of red earth mixed with crumbling bones found in the Hypogeum when it was first excavated, along with the enduring soil-marks on the walls in various rooms. It wouldn't account for the carefully buried intact skeletons on the Upper Level. Perhaps they were buried there later. Perhaps several explanations are necessary to understand the different kinds of interments in the Hypogeum and how it was used over time.

T. Eric Peet, writing soon after the discoveries, concludes: "It is quite clear that [the Hypogeum's] eventual fate was to be used as a burial place for thousands of individuals, but it is far from certain that this was the purpose for which it was built. The existence of the central chamber, with its careful work and laborious imitation of an open-air 'temple,' is against this interpretation. It has therefore been suggested that the hypogeum was meant for a burial place, and that the central chamber was the chapel or sanctuary in which the funeral rites were performed, after which the body was buried in one of the smaller rooms. This, however, does not explain the presence of burials in the chapel itself, and it is far more likely that it was only after Halsaflieni had ceased to be used for its original purpose that it was seized upon as a convenient place for burial."[37]

David Trump suggests that bodies were placed in side chambers, along with personal items.[38] As the community ran out of space, the skeletons would have been moved to make room for others. This went on for century after century, until approximately 7,000 people had been buried underground. In his opinion, the Middle Level would also have been used as a mortuary temple, perhaps as the site of funerary rituals. The Oracle Room, which is in the Middle Level, has side niches, which may have been used for burials.

A different scenario—which doesn't contradict but expands on these ideas—is that the Hypogeum was used for rites of personal transformation, including dream incubation. Perhaps people curled up on a small cot, like the "Sleeping Lady," or in a niche in the Main Chamber. Perhaps they prepared by watching swirling ochre patterns shift and change as they went deeper and deeper into a dreamlike state induced by incense, sound, and perhaps psychotropic preparations. Perhaps participants in an ancient Mystery School were initiated in the depths of the Hypogeum, a ritual that required lengthy time spent "buried" in darkness in the Earth.

And finally, what about the 7,000 bodies that were supposedly found in the initial excavation? Sir Themi Zammit extrapolated from a small sample; it seems likely that the resulting number was an exaggeration.

Second: What about the possibly-Paleolithic art found in the Hypogeum?

A bull fresco was located on the left wall of the Holy of Holies, in the Middle Level. This painting was in a style and done with a pigment that might have been pre-Neolithic, although not necessarily so.

The fresco was worthy of mention in David Trump's 1972 publication, *Malta: An Archaeological Guide*. He writes, "Before descending the stairs to the Lower Storey, visitors should pause to look at the wall opposite them. Dark lines of black paint outline what is apparently intended as a bull. It is crudely done, and the head and shoulders have not survived. That it is ancient and intentional is shown by the fact that the ochre wash on the wall ceases exactly at the black line. The bulls in relief at Tarxien ... offer parallels."[39] The painting is not mentioned in subsequent editions of his book, presumably because it was no longer there. When asked at a later date about the missing artwork, he apparently wasn't very concerned and said it had been quite faint anyway.[40]

The story we've heard is that the painting was erased by a staff-person in the 1990s, during a time when the Hypogeum was undergoing necessary renovations. Apparently, he was ordered to clean off mold from that part of the wall with a brush and water. Perhaps the painting was accidentally destroyed, and this fiasco was followed by a cover-up. Or perhaps the staff-person was ordered to get rid of the painting in order to obliterate proof of Paleolithic habitation on Malta—in other words, a cover-up. And what happened to the paint sample that, we are told, was sent out for analysis? We don't know.

Anton and Simon Mifsud describe other possible Paleolithic finds and other examples of Paleolithic art in the Hypogeum.[41] These include a hand print next to the Decorated Room and the black-and-white checkerboard design in the Main Chamber, in the Middle Level—not to mention the use of red ochre, which is chemically similar to the red pigment used in Paleolithic cave art and burials.

If these artistic examples are, indeed, Paleolithic, how could they have been painted on walls in a structure created between 3600–3000 BCE? Was the Middle Level actually an expansion and enlargement of limestone caves that were already there, just like the Upper Level? If so, and if there were humans on Malta prior to the Neolithic, they could have discovered these caves and made use of them—and left artistic evidence behind. If so, this art might have been honored and preserved by the later master builders.

Much is not known. Whether this constitutes a cover-up, a conspiracy, or a difference in opinion, we will let you decide.

Third: Elongated skulls?

There are stories about numerous, anomalous, elongated skulls being dug up in Ħal Saflieni Hypogeum by Fr. Magri in the early 1900s. One report was published in 1920 in *National Geographic Magazine* (Jan.–June, vol. XXXVII). T. Eric Peet writes in 1912 that 10 skulls were found in the excavations, and they were typical long-headed skulls, a type "usual among the neolithic races of the Mediterranean."[42]

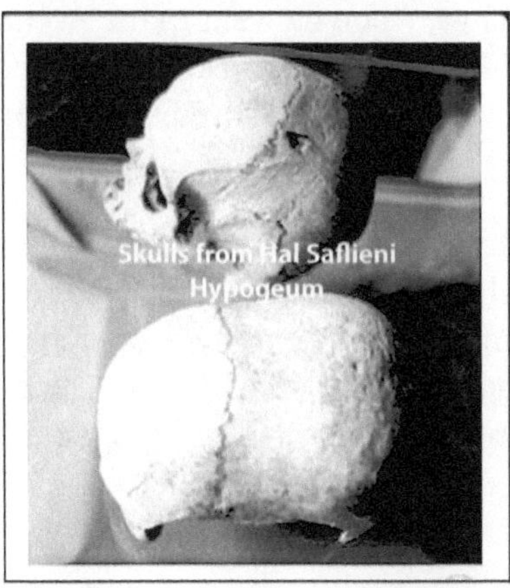

The references we have read on this topic describe elongated (dolichocephalic) skulls, some with additional unusual cranial features, including one that was completely lacking in the fossa median (the joint that goes up the top of the skull), which is supposed to be medically/anatomically impossible in a human. Similar anomalous skulls have been reportedly found in South America and Egypt.

A number of theories have developed to explain these long-headed skulls, including: they are evidence of a hither-to-unknown genetic mutation, of a hither-to-unknown human race, perhaps from Atlantis, or of a hither-to-unknown interbreeding with extra-terrestrials. Freddy Silva, for example, thinks the skulls provide evidence of an unusual, reclusive species of beings, perhaps priests, who lived on Malta.[43]

According to some sources, eleven [a number at odds with T. Eric Peet, who said there were only 10 skulls] of the skulls were on display in the Malta Museum of Archaeology in Valletta. Anton Mifsud and Charles Savona-Ventura took photos of them.[44] However, the skulls were removed from view in 1985 and are now only made available to selected researchers on special petition. Rumors have spread that five of the skulls have disappeared or have perhaps been stolen. According to Silva, when he went to the Archaeology Museum "armed" with photos of the skulls and requested to see them, his meeting with the Museum director was abruptly terminated.

Heritage Malta adamantly denies there is anything unusual about the skulls. They say the skulls are available for investigators to examine if they get the proper approval, but that there is nothing worth the effort to see. The recently revised (2017) multi-media display in the Hypogeum visitors' center makes a point to dismiss the topic, relegating it to the realm of absurd foolishness. Perhaps that is the proper realm for the topic. However, one could reasonably ask why, if there's nothing unusual about the skulls, they are no longer on display? Because exhibit space is scarce and the skulls are boring?

Unfortunately, Heritage Malta's strategy of ridicule and stonewalling has only encouraged conspiracy theorists. For a succinct summary, go to https://www.guidememalta.com/en/why-are-these-elongated-skulls-at-hal-saflieni-hypogeum-shrouded-in-mystery.[45]

Fourth: Missing school children?

There has been a persistent urban legend that in the late 1930s a group of school children and their teachers disappeared into the labyrinthian depths of the Hypogeum, never to be seen again. Although reported in reputable magazines, the story is considered a hoax by Heritage Malta. Of course, just because something is published in a reputable magazine doesn't necessarily mean that it is true.

The earliest published report of this "event" was in *National Geographic Magazine*, no. 78, 1940. In the article, Richard Walter writes that people used to be able to walk from one end of Malta to the other via subterranean tunnels and catacombs that opened out from the Hypogeum. However, government officials closed off access after a group of 30 school children and their teachers became lost and, apparently, died underground. These students were roped together, and the end secured to an entrance point. However, the rope was suddenly cut, and the walls collapsed, and they were buried. According to a different account, their desperate cries were heard for days as they wandered, lost, in the catacombs.

Some things are known for certain. Malta is made of limestone and riddled with underground caves. Some of these, such as the Hypogeum, have been expanded upon. It is not unlikely that tunnels were also built, and interconnected passageways could have existed. There are areas in the very lowest level of the Hypogeum that are no longer accessible. There is no published police report of "the missing school children incident"—an event that would have made local headlines and been thoroughly investigated by the local authorities.

Other than that, what is known? Was there an investigation that was "hushed up"? Were school children really lost, or was the story an "urban legend" to discourage people—especially children—from exploring subterranean passageways?

Fifth: Giant, white-haired humanoids?

Perhaps related to the "missing school children incident" (if it did occur) is another event that allegedly took place just a few weeks previously. A British woman named Lois Jessop visited the Hypogeum in the mid-1930s. According to her account, she and three others wandered off, with the permission of their guide, to investigate a burial chamber in the Lower Level "at their own risk."[46] She crawled through a passage and ended up on a two-foot-wide ledge in a huge cavern. Suddenly, twenty huge humanoid creatures covered with long white hair appeared out of an opening in the far wall. Not surprisingly, she was terrified. Something wet and slippery brushed past her and a sudden wind blew out her candle. She quickly retreated but, at the time, she didn't tell her companions what she had seen.

On her next visit to the Hypogeum, she found the passageway boarded up, and no-one appeared to know anything about her first guide. She realized that this was the same passageway where the walls had supposedly collapsed on the school group a few weeks after her visit.

Did Jessop really have an encounter with alien humanoids, or was this story her retroactive interpretation of a frightening incident caused by a sudden breeze blowing through the underground cavern? Her account has been discredited by some because she later went on to be very involved with UFO research. But perhaps that involvement was a direct outcome of her experience in the Hypogeum.

We leave it to you to draw your own conclusions. Elyn says that, given her own unsettling encounter with strange, translucent human-like beings dressed in white robes at Ġgantija Temple, she is not going to dismiss Jessop's experience out of hand.

At any rate, Jessop's account is an interesting description of what it was like to visit the Hypogeum before Heritage Malta developed it for "proper" tourism. If you want to explore this topic in greater detail, the following link provides a decent summary: https://www.guidememalta.com/en/stranger-things-the-mystery-of-the-lost-children-of-hal-saflieni-hy-pogeum.

Sixth: Offering pit or snake pit?

Some people have identified the pit where the "Sleeping Lady" was found in the Middle Level as a holy well where offerings were placed. Others (including Trump) have given it the name "The Snake Pit" and suggest it was a place where snakes were kept.

World-wide, the snake has been an important image of life and rebirth (it sheds its skin), of wisdom, healing, fertility—

and of the Mother/Earth Goddess, whose presence seems undeniable on Malta. A nearly 4-foot-long carving of a snake slithering up the side of a stone block was found in South Ġgantija Temple, and a dark crystalline vein that resembles a snake undulates across the limestone threshold stone at South Mnajdra Temple. You have to step over (or on) the crystalline snake to enter into the temple.

The temples are not the only places on Malta where one encounters snakes. According to legend, when St. Paul was shipwrecked on Malta he was bitten by a poisonous snake that sprung out of the kindling being used to feed a bonfire. He should have dropped dead immediately, but the viper didn't kill him. This miraculous event demonstrated to the local pagans that St. Paul was a very powerful religious person, and he was able to begin converting them to Christianity. Apparently, he also "converted" the poisonous snakes and insects, since there are no venomous snakes or insects on Malta—but neither is there any indication that there ever were. One might wonder whether the legend is actually a metaphorical description of St. Paul "conquering" the Earth Mother.

Seventh: Acoustical effects and oracles?

Although many writers believe the sound effect in the Oracle Room was intentional, others scoff and consider it an unintentional byproduct of construction. For example, Anthony Pace, author of the Heritage Malta Insight Guide, The Ħal Saflieni Hypogeum, states that "Modern myth would have us believe that the niche was imbued with special acoustic qualities that were once used by an oracle."[47] It is not clear if Pace is discounting the acoustic effects or the idea of an oracle. David Trump concludes that "The reverberations of the Oracle Room may well have played a part here [in religious ceremonies]."[48]

We don't know if any oracular rituals were practiced by the ancient Maltese. Perhaps their religious specialists used the powerful vibrational effect of the oracle hole to alter consciousness as part of initiation or mortuary rituals; perhaps they used it to increase their perceived spiritual power. Or maybe they did use it for oracular purposes. Oracular practices go back millennia and are found all over the world.

Mnajdra, Ħaġar Qim, and Tarxien Temples also have so-called oracle holes. These are carefully carved openings that pierce from one more-public chamber to a less-public one. These may or may not have had acoustical qualities. Some may have had astronomical alignments.

Thanks to the emerging discipline of archaeo-acoustics, we know that thousands of years ago people throughout the world selected and modified sites for their acoustical properties—including Paleolithic cave artists. So why not the skilled master builders of the Hypogeum?

Tarxien Temples, Paola, central Malta — Sophisticated stonework, spiral designs, animal reliefs, and a massive obese guardian

Tarxien (tar-sheen) Temples are included in the UNESCO list of World Heritage Sites. Anthony Pace considers them "the most complex of Malta's megalithic structures in terms of layout and internal embellishments."[49] The surviving Tarxien artwork is varied and impressive, and much of it is unlike artwork found elsewhere on Malta (or anywhere else).

Tarxien Temples are about 1/4 mile due east from Ħal Saflieni Hypogeum. In prehistoric times, one could probably see the above-ground megalithic structures of the Hypogeum from Tarxien and vice versa. They appear to be paired, just like Ġgantija Temples and Xagħra Circle/Hypogeum, and to be the same distance apart. Each hypogeum is located to the west of its respective temples, suggesting a relationship with death and the setting sun.

David Trump says "This is the most complex of all temple sites in Malta..."[50] Along with complexity, the temples are noteworthy because the richest deposit of prehistoric art objects on the island has been found here.

Tarxien Temples have given their name to the last Temple Period phase, which dates from 3000–2500 BCE, although their location was in use perhaps as early as 4100 BCE. The four Tarxien Temples were constructed between 3600–2500 BCE. After the end of the Temple Period, they were repurposed, first by Early Bronze-Age settlers who used them for both crematorium and cemetery, and later by Phoenician, Punic, and Roman settlers. It appears that all these ancient people recognized that Tarxien was a very powerful place.

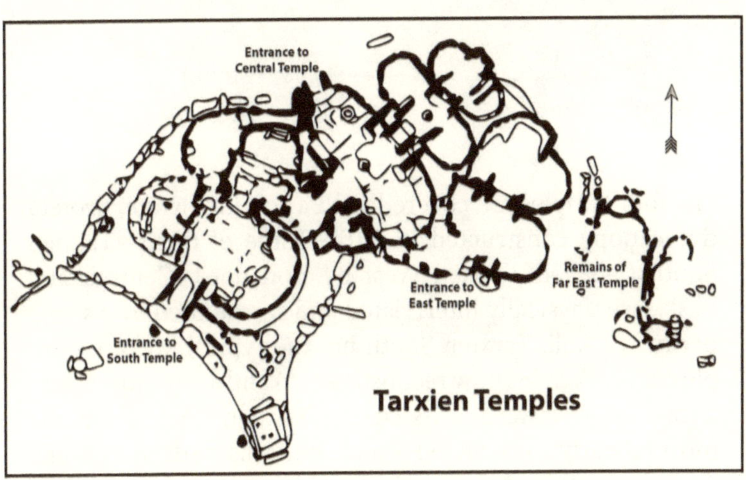

The first excavation took place in 1915, two years after a farmer had informed Sir Themi Zammit, Malta's museum curator, about unusual stones he had found in his fields. Today, Tarxien Temples are situated in a relatively green oasis, surrounded by a high stone wall and urban buildings, next to a modern cemetery.

The four temples are covered with a soaring, white, protective canopy constructed in 2014. Three of them—Tarxien South (labelled Tarxien West by Bonanno), Central, and East—are physically interrelated and surrounded by a single perimeter wall. Tarxien South has the typical Maltese temple curved façade (now reconstructed) and a large forecourt, with a water cistern at its center. Tarxien Central was the most recently constructed temple and was wedged between Tarxien South and Tarxien East, which is the smallest of the three. Tarxien Far East is a separate, five-apse temple and the oldest. It is in quite poor repair. All of the temples were altered and remodeled over the centuries, with entire walls in the western half of the South Temple being dismantled at some point.

Reconstructed obese
person statue

A raised walkway with handrails encircles the perimeter, and another set of walkways with handrails leads the visitor through each of the temples in turn. There are numerous descriptive plaques and you can see many of the interior rooms from the walkways, although you can't enter most of them.

In 1956 most of the original altars, decorated slabs, and benches in Tarxien South and Tarxien Central were moved to the National Museum of Archaeology in Valletta for safekeeping from the elements and vandalism. They have been replaced on-site with replicas. A few original sculptures are still housed in the small visitors' center/ticket office on the site. Even though the visitor will see a number of reconstructions and replacements instead of original stonework, wandering through the complex maze of rooms is an impressive—and even powerful—experience.

Tarxien East was built during the same time period as Tarxien South. Even though it is much plainer, it has extremely well-cut slab walls and two oracles holes. The floors of its four apses are made of *torba*. There is a flight of steps between Tarxien East and Tarxien Central. Now these stairs go nowhere, but at one time they led to an upper chamber or the roof.

Tarxien Central is the only Maltese temple to have been built with a six-apse plan. It is generally considered the masterpiece of Maltese temple-building because of its highly sophisticated stone work and building techniques. The pavement of part of the Central Temple is formed by huge flat megaliths, apparently needed to bring the Central Temple to the same level as the West and East Temples. A giant stone cauldron, carved from a single piece of stone, stands in the first apse to the left as you enter the Central Temple. Its use is unknown.

A low (replica) stone block with two carved spirals obstructs the entrance into the second set of apses, and thus, also, into the third, innermost set of apses. Perhaps the elevated threshold served as a physical and symbolic barrier between sacred and even more sacred space. Anthropologist Marija Gimbutas thinks the spiral oculi (two spirals, turning in opposite directions) represent the eyes of the Goddess and "serve to partition corridors and chambers in the [Maltese] temples, accentuating the presence of the Goddess."[51] [Note: A large stone carved with similar spiral oculi was found at the Temple of Artemis Ephesia, Empúries, Catalonia, Spain—indication that the pattern continued to be popular (and perhaps meaningful) millennia later.]

Some of the orthostats are heavily reddened, indication that a fire destroyed part of the building.

On either side of the central passage behind this low, spiral-decorated stone block, at the entrances to the middle two apses, are two (replica) limestone screens, ca. 55" high. They are decorated with four spirals, carved in relief over a rhythmically pitted background. There is a small stone hearth in the center passage, discolored from burning.

The left apse at the rear of Tarxien Central has remarkably tight-fitting upright slabs, indicative of very skilled stone craftsmanship. There is a suggestion in the remaining stonework that this apse was covered by a corbelled roof or an arched dome.

In a small room between the South and Central Temples are large relief carvings of two horned bulls facing each other.

Below them is a carving of what might be a sow with 13 piglets. It is possible that the 13 piglets refer to the annual cycle of the moon. A hollow pit covered with a stone plug was recently discovered in this room. Again, we can only wonder about the significance.

Tarxien South has an imposing (concrete reconstruction) trilithon entrance and façade. It "was distinguished by a series of rock carvings that to this day make up one of the most important repertoires of art works known from world prehistory."[52] It has four apses, two each on either side of a central passageway. There is an elevated niche at the back. It also has niches or small alcoves within the thickness of the walls. During the final stage of development of Tarxien, one of the chambers in this temple was modified to provide access to the more-recently-constructed Central Temple.

A colossal Globigerina Limestone statue stood guard or perhaps greeted the visitor in the first apse on the right in Tarxien South. The statue has been severely damaged, probably by agricultural equipment, but what is left of it, from tiny feet to ample waist, is 43" high. The upper torso is gone, but originally it may have been 9' high. The statue has the typical little feet, balloon-like calves, and short skirt/kilt of other obese statues. This giant statue is often referred to as a Goddess statue. The replica in this location has been reconstructed so that it has an intact right hip, leg, and foot.

This same apse also holds a hollow altar decorated with pairs of oculi-like spirals turning in opposite directions. A stone plug closed access to the interior. When the plug was removed in 1915, archaeologists discovered a beautiful, 4" long, curved flint knife placed on top of a collection of small animal bones, flint flakes, goat's horns, snail shells, and a stone spatula and ceramic fragments. This might suggest animal sacrifice was practiced here.

The first left apse of the South Temple is equally elaborate but quite different. It includes several upright standing stones, spiral-decorated altars, and two spiral-decorated, horizontal stone blocks, 6' long, whose position appears to mimic the external concave façade. It also contains two limestone slabs with animal relief carvings. One narrow, broken limestone frieze now measures 44" in length. Four carved horned animals (probably sheep or goats), a very well-fed pig, and possibly a ram parade across the limestone from left to right. The other stone frieze is 66" long and consists of two rows of 11 sheep or goats, facing to the left. Do they represent symbolic (or actual) sacrifices? Do they represent gratitude or hope for healthy, prolific flocks, a kind of "positive affirmation" carved in limestone? We can only guess.

Crude boat graffiti were scratched by a different population than the temple builders onto orthostats in this apse, possibly during the Early Bronze Age, after 2500 BCE. Perhaps the artists were asking for help with their catch, or aid in trade, or for a safe journey. Perhaps they were recording successful voyages or the arrival of a foreign fleet.

A variety of human sculptures were found in the Tarxien Temples, including a number of clay and stone heads of different styles. There are various small, obese statuettes and statues without heads. Perhaps some of the heads were intended to be placed on the headless torsos. There is a rough clay statuette, 1" high, of two people embracing. Another rough clay figure, 2.3" high, looks like a pregnant woman holding her head with one hand and pointing to her swollen vulva with the other. A small, headless, sitting clay figurine, only 1.5" high, has her knees drawn up to her ample hips and breasts. The lower half of a severely damaged, seated stone statuette has smaller figures lined up under the bottom of the statue's skirt. Did these represent children? Worshippers?

A carved limestone slab (approx. 10" high) with two upright phalli enclosed in a niche, with traces of red ochre and a pitted base, was found at Tarxien, as was another one (4.7" high) of three upright phalli side by side.

A broken, hollow, terracotta standing figurine (approx. 24" high) with a solemn expression was also found here. It may represent a priest or priestess (the chest and right arm are missing), with a wig-like hairstyle and a long pleated skirt. Some researchers assume the figurine is a priest, either because they assume religious figures were male or because, since it isn't obese, it must be male. Gender bias runs both ways in the interpretation of these enigmatic figures.

A number of spiral patterns are carved in bas-relief on limestone blocks and altars in Tarxien (and at some other temples). These varied, complex spiral designs have become widely commercialized images. They call to mind the well-known Irish Newgrange triple-spiral motif, which dates back to 3200 BCE—the same time period as Tarxien Temples.

Spiral designs found in Tarxien Temples include linked pairs turning in opposite directions; double tiers of interconnected spirals with what appear to be spikes, or tendrils, or buds protruding from the spiral coils; and twirling, vine-like spirals. There are numerous variations on these repetitive patterns. Some spiral designs are geometrical, but some are organic and vegetal, reminding one of the swirling "tree of life" found painted on a ceiling at nearby Ħal Saflieni Hypogeum.

It is interesting to compare the Tarxien spirals with the much-more free-flowing and impressionistic ochre spirals painted on the walls and ceilings of the Hypogeum. Perhaps the locations in which the artists worked resulted in different artistic expressions. It would be much easier to carefully plot out a pattern on a stone block than on an undulating cave roof and easier to sculpt in daylight than paint in dim, flickering lamplight. Perhaps the different media also lent themselves to a different aesthetic. Or perhaps, the artists had different intentions.

In addition to the above art and sculpture, a number of ceramic and stone pots, bowls, and containers of different shapes and sizes were also found in Tarxien Temples. Many of them are decorated, some with cross-hatching, others with curving lines, some with the addition of dot-like bosses. Some of them may have been used for ritual ablutions or libations, but we don't know. A number of puzzling conical stones have also been found, along with a 15" high, fragmented model of a temple façade that has been reconstructed and provides important information on construction methods.

Early Bronze-Age artifacts have been found in the cremation cemetery that was dug at a later date into the existing temple complex. These finds include ceramic vessels, copper axes and daggers, and figurines that clearly show Greek and Sicilian artistic influence.

Our Experience at Tarxien

Elyn's Experience: I found it hard at first to experience Tarxien. First of all, we circumambulated it from a raised walkway, looking down on multiple chambers and corridors. The layout of the temples was easier to see this way, but the physical distance resulted in an energetic distance as well.

Then a tour group arrived and gathered together before the impressive (replica) trilithon entrance to the West Temple. The leader was dressed in a loose, flowing white gown and had flowers woven into her long dark hair. The "priestess" effect was a little diminished by her raincoat, but it was clear what role she was enacting. She began to organize an "entering in to sacred space" ritual. Her group of a dozen men and women formed a line, and one by one they paused, raised their arms, and walked through the impressive entryway. Even from a distance, I could sense their excited buzz.

I wondered what ritual they were performing. Did they think they were using this powerful place the same way the ancient

Maltese did? If so, how could they possibly know? Or were they knowingly using this sacred site for their own newly constructed spiritual practices—co-opting the temple, just as sacred sites have been co-opted for millennia?

I felt conflicted. I wanted to go into the temple myself, but now I felt hesitant to enter into what had become their sacred space. At the same time, I was glad to see people moving into the temple with conscious awareness that they were entering a powerful place. It reminded me to use the BLESSING practice before I walked on this sacred ground.

Gary's Experience: I was filled with intellectual curiosity about the carvings, the extensive spaces, the pit that was recently discovered. But I didn't get a big "hit."

Entry Information

The site is controlled by Heritage Malta, http://heritage-malta.org. The Heritage Malta Multisite Pass gives access to Tarxien Temples.

Getting There

Tarxien Temples are located in Paola, Malta, fairly close to Valletta and to the airport. Regular buses stop in the main square in Paola. Tarxien is about a ten-minute walk from the bus stop. Walk along Church Avenue straight up to the T-intersection with Neolithic Temples Street and turn right. Malta Sightseeing "Hop On Hop Off" South/Red buses stop at Tarxien Temples and the Hypogeum. The Hypogeum is about a 15-minute walk.

Controversies

Spirals

What do the spirals signify? Scholars have made numerous suggestions based on their modern construction of meaning and, sometimes, on historical descriptions of ancient symbology. Interpretations include eternity, rebirth, renewal, growth, solar events, an "oculus" (round, eye-like) motif to ward off intruders, harmony, and expansion. Marija Gimbutas says the spirals "may symbolize the energies of plants and snakes, and the cyclical regeneration of life."[53] Francis Aloisio thinks "the temple builders used them in their structures to harmonize energy. Spirals were expression of electromagnetic currents and are the symbol of change."[54]

Cheryl Straffon writes, "The Earth was the Goddess that grew the tree, and the branches were the spirals that gave the fruit to nourish the people. When the spirals were carved next to each other, this represented continuity of life and beyond that reincarnation. The spirals could also have represented the coils of a snake."[55]

Without an eye-witness account from the Maltese master builders, it is impossible to know what the different spirals meant to them. What we can say, however, is that is what the spirals mean to Gimbutas, Aloisio, and Straffon.

Ahead of their time?

When Anthony Bonanno describes the possible corbelled ceiling in Tarxien Central, he adds that it is "precocious" that the builders could have "come to grips with the principle of the vertical arch and of the dome structure."[56] He also goes on to comment, "Equally astonishing for a prehistoric society, still lacking the sophisticated hierarchical structure typical of the 'civilizations' of the eastern Mediterranean, is the temple people's achievement in the field of sculpture and ceramic art."[57]

Although Bonanno seems to be praising the ancient Maltese, his comments need to be re-examined. Bonanno's observation exposes his unconscious bias that artistic development requires hierarchy and, presumably, the competition and warfare that is associated with the eastern Mediterranean "civilizations" such as Crete or Mycenae.

The Maltese temple builders stand out as an early and noteworthy exception to those assumptions. They appear to have been a peaceful society with minimal hierarchy. Centralized communal burials did not preserve status and separation. Although there was probably a priesthood, and specialist artists and master builders, there does not appear to be other evidence of marked class structure and differentiation.

Speaking about the complex spiral patterns found carved into limestone blocks at Tarxien, Sharon Sultana says, "The precision of these spirals almost gives us the impression that the designs were measured before being carved."[58] As if these master builders, capable of planning complex stone constructions and aligning temples to astronomical events, didn't know how to make measurements? Her statement is also indicative of unconscious bias.

Orientations

Tarxien Temples appear to be oriented more or less to the southwest, the direction of the winter solstice sunset. Klaus Albrecht states that he doesn't know why the orientation was toward sunset instead of sunrise, but it clearly was.[59] Based on the precession of Sirius, Lenie Reedijk gives the following dates for the four Tarxien Temples: Tarxien Far East (which she calls Tarxien Early) was built to face the rising of Sirius in around 9050 BCE; Tarxien East was built to face the setting of Sirius in 8550 BCE; Tarxien Central (Middle) was built to face the setting of Sirius in 4850 BCE; and Tarxien West (South) was built to face the setting of Sirius in 8300 BCE.[60] Reedijk has some interesting ideas about why and how Tarxien Central was constructed between the two other temples.[61]

Ħaġar Qim and Mnajdra Temples, near Qrendi, Malta — Powerful places with astronomical alignments

Ħaġar Qim (adge-ar eem or adge-ar qeem) and Mnajdra (mm-nigh-dra) Temples are located in an idyllic setting on the southern coast of Malta, overlooking the Mediterranean. Ħaġar Qim means "Standings Stones" or "Stones of Veneration," an indication that the site's importance was never forgotten. High-tech protective canopies were installed in 2009 to protect Mnajdra and Ħaġar Qim from the rain, sun, and wind. Built between 4000–2500 BCE (Ħaġar Qim is the elder), they are UNESCO World Heritage Sites.

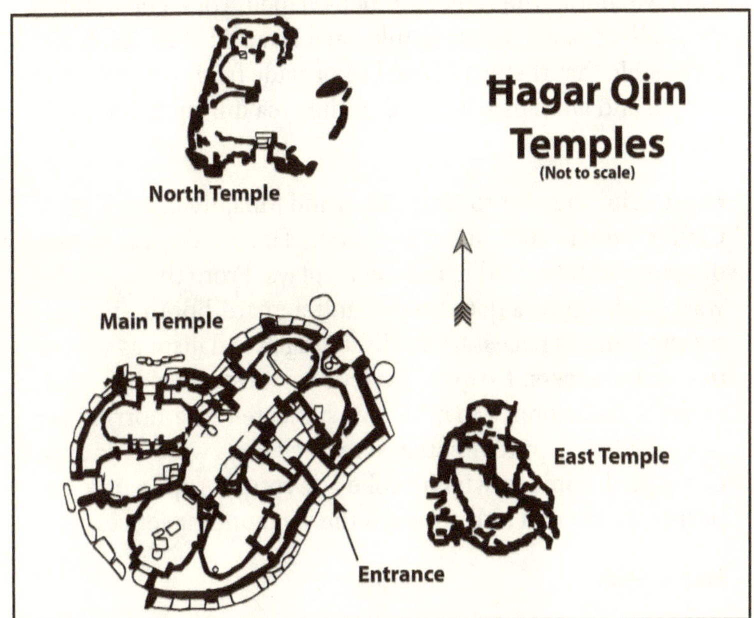

Isolated from the busy buzz of modern urban life, the temples offer an opportunity to experience sacred sites in a natural setting in relative peace and quiet. Perhaps this ambiance (if one can disregard the soaring white canopies) is more like what the ancient Maltese experienced at these powerful places—but perhaps it isn't.

The two sets of temples are "twinned," like many of the other temples we have described. Ħaġar Qim Temples are located at the crest of a ridge that slopes away on all sides; Mnajdra Temples are 1/3 mile southeast and downhill from Ħaġar Qim, closer to the sea and above the southern cliffs. They are intervisible. The tiny island of Filfla, once used for bombing practice by the British and NATO, is visible from Mnajdra. So far, no one has discovered a hypogeum or cemetery associated with these temples.

The Misqa Tanks are located at the top of the hill 1/6 mile from Mnajdra. The tanks are bell-shaped, rock-cut cisterns that collect rainwater. It is unknown how old they are, but it is possible that they were used to provide fresh water for the people and animals who lived in the area during the Temple Period.

One begins the visit to Ħaġar Qim and Mnajdra at the Visitor Center, built in 2008. It has a number of interesting multi-media presentations and hands-on displays. From there, a sidewalk leads up to a gated fence and a guard booth. The unsightly fence is necessary to discourage vandalism as well as to control access. Despite the fence, on Good Friday, 2001, under a full moon, Mnajdra was subjected to a horrific act of vandalism. Approximately sixty megaliths were dislodged or toppled, some of which broke as a result. Apparently, the perpetrators cut a hole through the surrounding fence.

Ħaġar Qim

Millennia after it was abandoned, the massive Globigerina Limestone megaliths of Ħaġar Qim still protruded through the accumulated soil and debris that had buried much of the site. A number of paintings, engravings, lithographs, and watercolors show Ħaġar Qim as it appeared from the 1780s–1890s. Some of these have provided visual aids to help archaeologists in reconstructing the temple. Mnajdra was apparently less visible or less impressive; at any rate, no depictions have been discovered.

An early excavation of Ħaġar Qim Temples was undertaken in 1839 and another in 1840. It was thought at the time that the temples were Phoenician in origin because no one thought that anything so old—however old it was, no one was sure—could have been built by the ancient, indigenous Maltese. Sir Temi Zammit and T. Eric Peet carried out further, much more rigorous excavations in 1909. Other excavations followed. However, it was not until the application of carbon dating techniques in the 1960s that the earliest construction date—4000 BCE—was established for the temples, 3000 years before the arrival of the Phoenicians on Malta.

Ħaġar Qim Temples are 109 yards from the Visitor Center and is visible from it. The four megalithic structures are at a slightly higher elevation. The massive Main Building is best preserved, but there are also two smaller outlying buildings to the north and east, and a group of megaliths to the west.

Walking from the Visitor Center, one arrives first at the East Building. It consists of a number of irregular rooms whose functions are not known.

Next, one reaches the Main Building. It was constructed, expanded, and changed repeatedly during the many centuries it was in use. As a result, it has an unusual, irregular, and complicated floorplan with blocked-off entryways and chambers accessible only through the perimeter wall. The Main Building may have begun as a more or less regular four- or five-apse temple, but its current shape leaves much in doubt.

To adequately visualize the layout of this complicated and often-altered temple, a detailed floor plan is required.[62] And even that isn't sufficient to understand how the different interior spaces were actually used.

The Main Building's monumental concave façade faces southeast and is approached via a paved oval forecourt. The massive upright stones in the perimeter wall make a powerful impression on the visitor, even though many are heavily eroded. A second course of megalithic stones is laid over the first, increasing the height of the wall above the trilithon entryway. A stone bench runs along the length of the façade. The front of Ħaġar Qim resembles the small temple-façade model found at Tarxien.

Wind and rain, along with corrosive salt spray, have caused much damage to the relatively soft Globigerina Limestone perimeter wall, but its looming megaliths are still quite impressive. The tallest remaining megalith is 15' or 17' high, depending on who was measuring, and projects like a huge gnarled finger above the wall. One of the largest megaliths, found in the perimeter wall behind the right-hand corner of the façade, measures 21' long x 17' high and weighs approximately 20 tons. One has to wonder how the ancient master builders were able to transport and erect such mammoth stones. As at other temples, the space between the exterior wall and the interior walls was filled with soil and rubble.

One enters through the imposing trilithon into a passageway. There is a chamber (or apse) on either side. The two chambers are accessible through off-set porthole slab entries—upright slab-like stones with a very large opening carved out of the center, creating a frame-like entrance. Perhaps the chambers were originally screened off with some kind of material. A free-standing altar and a horizontal stone block decorated with pitting and spiral oculi were found in this entry passage. They have been replaced by replicas. The original altar is in the National Museum of Archeology, Valletta; the original stone block is in the Visitor Center.

The visitor continues past these apses into a long, oval space oriented toward the left. On the right is another apse. An elliptical hole in its interior wall and an opening behind a niche in the perimeter wall appear to function together to mark the summer-solstice sunrise.

Standing in the long, oval space, one has access to four additional chambers or apses. Directly ahead, there is also an exit to (or entry from) the outside, like the back door in a building. This entrance/exit gives access to the four interior chambers and to shrines and niches accessible from outside, without having to enter through the main trilithon.

The oval space contains several constructions that archaeologists refer to as altars. A set of three steps in the southern corner of the oval space leads up to another chamber, which has a cylindrical stone pillar inside. Each apse or chamber is different, and the entryways vary from a small opening, blocked off by low stone slabs, to porthole-slab doorways. Most of them contain one or more altars and/or several niches.

Various inward-slanting ("over-sailing") horizontal courses of stones suggest that some of the apses were originally covered with a corbelled roof. Evidence of this same "false-vault" technique is found in other Maltese temples, and it was used a thousand years later in Mycenae.

The northernmost chamber is only accessible from the outside, through an entrance in the external wall. Also in the external wall is a niche with a megalithic pillar and a triangular slab. It is most unusual—in fact, unique—to have such an important ritual feature on the outside of a Maltese temple. A severely damaged statue of what appears to have been two standing figures can be seen in the external wall of the southwest chamber. It is vaguely reminiscent, though much larger, of the two-seated-people figurine found in Xagħra Circle/Hypogeum.

A number of altar-like constructions were found, some on pedestals, some flanking the doorway to a chamber. One intriguing, free-standing altar (or table) was discovered in the entry passageway. Each of the four sides of this altar has a relief carving of what appears to be a tall, narrow plant growing from a vessel, though it could represent horns or ribs and a basket instead. The vessel is topped with two loops that might be handles or might represent the eyes of a deity. There are 10–12 leaves on each side of the central trunk or stem. Decoratively pitted pillars enclose either side of the plant/tree. The rest of the altar is also pitted.

A total of 14 figurines were found in the Main Building. A number of seated obese stone figurines were found in the first apses; similar obese figurines, some standing, were found under the steps leading up to the elevated chamber. Most of them have their arms crossed below their bellies or their left hand resting in the folds of their waists and their right hand pointing down. They range in size from 8" to 30" high. Most are quite small, but several are larger and stand upright, one on a decorative, pitted base. None of them appear to have breasts, and none of them have heads, although they were constructed with a hole into which a head could be inserted. Perhaps different heads were used at different times of year, or to represent different personages or genders. We wonder if the statues were ritually "decommissioned" before being buried, since no heads have been found in association with them.

A small, 5" tall clay standing nude figurine dubbed the "Venus of Ħaġar Qim" or "The Venus of Malta" because of her ample, pendulous breasts was also found in the first apses. Providing dramatic stylistic contrast with the obese statuettes, the Venus of Ħaġar Qim is quite naturalistic. Like other statuettes, however, her left arm is bent and her right arm points down toward her legs. Like the other figures, she has no head.

100

A small pottery fragment found at Ħaġar Qim seems to show a solar wheel divided into eight sections. Each wedge has a dot inside, and the surrounding circle is marked with what look like the rays of the sun.[63]

Leaving the Main Building behind, the visitor can see the remains of the North Temple 100' to the north. It originally had four or five apses, but only the left and central have survived. At the far end is a polygonal niche and a stone pillar. West of the North Temple are the West Remains, an irregular group of dislocated megaliths.

What conclusions can be drawn from Ħaġar Qim's complicated layout? Katya Stroud points out that "A number of architectural elements in the temples appear to dictate visual and at times even physical access in these buildings, making it apparent that movement through them and participation in the activities they housed was somewhat restricted."[64] In addition, it appears that ritual activities were not only conducted inside the Main Building but also in the space outside, in openings in the perimeter wall surrounding it, and in nearby smaller buildings.

Heritage Malta organizes Summer Solstice Sunrise events at Ħaġar Qim. Tickets are limited and must be purchased in advance at http://heritagemalta.org.

Our experience at Ħaġar Qim

Elyn's Experience: I stared at the stipple-dimple-pecked designs on one of the stone slabs and began to get dizzy. The Flower of Life pattern formed before my eyes. My companion saw honeycombs. I wondered if it was simply a "brain game" of making sense out of randomness, drawing lines between dots, but I found it only occurred on certain slabs and not on others... I think it was intentional, a technique for altering consciousness. Imagine: the temple is roofed over; it's dark inside but lit in certain spots by flickering lamplight that casts shadows...the pecked patterns begin to shift and move....

Mnajdra

Mnajdra Temples are "twinned" with Ħaġar Qim, but they are not twinned in layout or appearance. Unlike Ħaġar Qim, Mnajdra is constructed of a mixture of soft Globigerina and harder Coralline Limestone. And also unlike Ħaġar Qim Temples, Mnajdra Temples have retained a coherent layout and contain extensive examples of mesmerizing pitted decoration. They also have a series of significant astronomical alignments. The temples look to the sea, but they also look toward the rising sun.

Mnajdra is made up of three temples—the Lower, Central, and East Temples—accessed across a common paved forecourt 100' across. Groups of stone to the east may have constituted additional buildings or enclosures. Pottery found at Mnajdra indicates that the area was in use as early as 4100 BCE. The three-apse Upper (East) Temple is the oldest, dating to 3600–3200 BCE. The Central Temple is the most recent and dates to the later Tarxien Phase (3150–2500 BCE). The Lower (South) Temple—"one of the most impressive megalithic architecture one can find in the Maltese islands"—dates to around 3200 BCE. The rear exterior walls of the South and Central Temples are constructed of Coralline Limestone, using the same "header-and-stretcher" technique used at Ġgantija Temples.

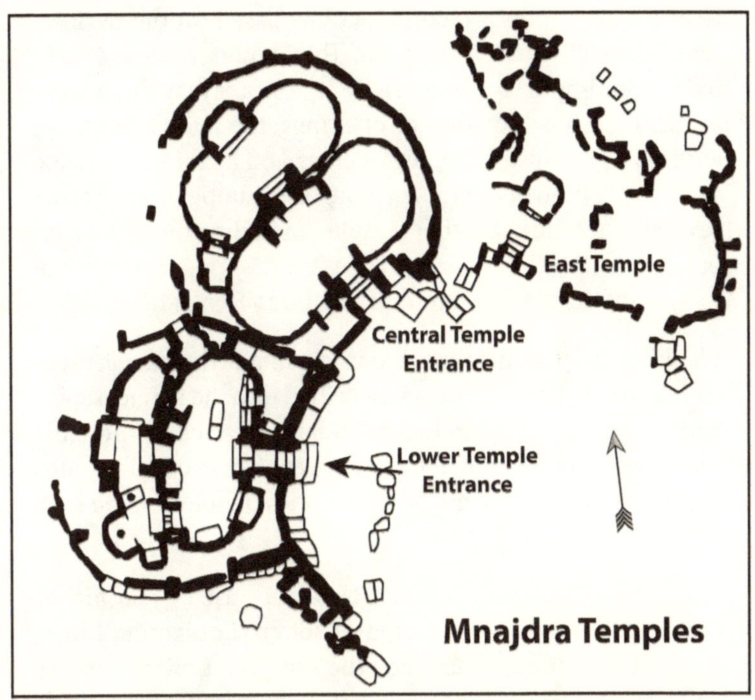

Walkways with rope railings guide the visitor through the temples and limit access to most of the chambers, including the altar at the rear of the Lower Temple. Apparently, this has been done to protect the stones and the temple structure; however, it also makes it more difficult to experience these sacred sites.

The East Temple: The oldest Mnajdra temple is a simple trefoil (three-lobe) design. It is constructed of Coralline Limestone and appears to have a small altar in the back niche. It is oriented toward the southwest and the tiny island of Filfla. Why that alignment was important is not known, but perhaps Filfla was used as a ceremonial site. Richard England suggests "that the altar-like shape or bulls' horns profile of the islet attracted the attention of the temple builders."[65]

Its walls are modern reconstructions based on the perimeter of the still-extant *torba* floor. The number three seems to have been important here, since it appears that there were originally three doorways or openings; the temple has three apses; and the apse at the rear is closed off by three low stone slabs with pitted decoration. [Note: the number three occurs several other times at other temples, including the triple altar in Ġgantija South's inner left apse and the triple entry in the temple model graffito found in Mnajdra's Central Temple.]

Flanking the rear apse are two intriguing orthostats. Irregular horizontal lines of dots were drilled into the surfaces, perhaps representing a kind of calendar or star chart, possibly recording "the dates of heliacal risings of stars or star groups starting with the Pleiades."[66] These lines of holes can be seen from the walkway.

The Central (Middle) Temple: This four-apse (+ rear niche) building is mostly constructed of softer Globigerina Limestone. It was inserted between the East and Lower Temples and is oriented southeast. It is slightly raised on an artificial platform. The main access is through what was once an impressive porthole-slab entrance; two megaliths form a passage in front of it. The Central Temple appears to have two entries, side by side. It has impressive megalithic stones topped with a double course of vertical stones, indicative of a corbelled roof.

A graffito of a temple façade is visible on the right vertical megalith in the first south apse. One wonders who carved it there and why. There is a small shrine in the back apse of the temple. Astronomical alignments at the solstices and equinoxes have been suggested, but David Trump argues against this: "The fact that at midsummer a much broader splodge of light hits the left hand upright at no particularly significant point rather spoils the argument..."[67] However, recent research indicates without doubt that the Central Temple is oriented to the winter solstitial sunrise.[68]

The Lower (South) Temple: This temple is noteworthy not only for its setting but also for its largely intact façade and extended external bench, mesmerizing pitted decoration, two-level altar niches, and multiple, indisputable solar alignments.

The visitor enters the four-apse Lower Temple through a large trilithon doorway that opens directly east. The threshold is worth noticing: a dark crystalline mineral vein undulates across the lighter limestone. It resembles a snake and was surely chosen intentionally for that location. What this means, however, we can only guess. A reference to the Goddess? To rebirth? We can look to other cultures in which snakes have religious significance, but we really don't know what they meant to the ancient Maltese.

The temple has four apses, two on either side of a central axis, as well as a chamber accessed from the apse to the right of the entrance. The first two apses (we'll call them 1 and 2) are divided from the two inner apses (3 and 4) by a trilithon. At the end of the central axis is what appears to be an altar. In 2012 we were able to approach the altar, but access has since been restricted.

When one enters the temple, one sees an eye-dazzling assortment of pitted/pecked stones and trilithon entryways. Apse 1, on the left, has a niche and a portal doorway-within-in-trilithon entrance in its west wall, leading into apse 3.

To the right is apse 2. It has a number of interesting features, including what appear to be benches along the curving wall and several upright pitted megaliths near the central trilithon that leads into the inner apses. If one turns around to face the entrance, one will see three steps in the east-facing interior wall that lead into a small chamber accessed via a porthole slab.

Apse 2 has two oracle holes that open into interior spaces. Tore Lomsdalen has measured the alignment of these holes and found that one is directed towards the Summer Solstice Sunrise, the other towards the Winter Solstice Sunrise. He suggests the oracle holes may have been related to seasonal rituals and ceremonies "occurring at the sun's most northern and southern positions on the horizon, at the spring and autumn equinox, or at other special times related to astronomical events and their cosmology."[69]

Apse 3 is accessed (or was, since it is now off-limits) through apse 1. The entrance is composed of two doorways: a trilithon, behind which is a porthole, flanked with two tapered vertical slabs. All are completely covered with densely pitted designs. Inside apse 3 are two double-tiered altars, one directly ahead of the entrance and the other to the left. It appears a third altar, now collapsed, was on the right in apse 3.

Apse 4 is slightly higher than the other apses. A roughly modeled clay figurine (2" high) and suggestive twists of clay were found during excavations in 1910 under the floor. The figure appears to represent a seated pregnant woman with truncated legs and arms, a huge belly, and equally exaggerated breasts.

A number of the stones in the Lower Temple are profusely decorated with typical Maltese pitted decoration. Although the pockmarks may have been made at random, they appear to form swirling, curving patterns and might have served (perhaps with the aid of flickering lamplight) as a way to alter states of consciousness.

There is evidence that parts of the Lower Temple were covered. The northern wall of apse 2 is topped with horizontal stone courses that slope inwards. Presumably the opening would originally have been closed with a corbelled roof.

Astronomical alignments: The Lower Temple was precisely oriented so that its central axis aligns exactly due east. On the days of the spring and autumn equinoxes (ca. March 21 and September 21), the sun rises exactly due east and set exactly due west. This divides day and night into equal parts. The sun rises behind a hill, and then a beam of sunlight travels down the central corridor in the Lower Temple and shines onto the altar at the end. The bottom of the lintel of the trilithon entryway casts a shadow on the wall behind the altar; this assures that the sun appears to rise not much higher than the altar top.

A different sunrise arrangement occurs for the summer and winter solstices (ca. June 21 and December 21). On these occasions, the sun passes through a thin slit formed by megaliths at the entrance to the Lower Temple and shines onto one (or the other) of the two large, pecked, upright stones placed on each side of the trilithon that leads to the inner apses. These two orthostats are slightly larger at the top than bottom, separated from the trilithon by another set of orthostats. There is a stone seat or bench in front of each of these.

The cross-quarter days (February 1, May 1, August 1, and November 1) are also marked by the sun shining onto either the two decorated orthostats on either side of the inner tri-lithon or onto the set of stones and benches directly to the left and right of the trilithon. The system is both complicated and ingenious.[70]

Heritage Malta allows access to Mnajdra Temples for these astronomical events (see information below). Being present at these seasonal cyclical occurrences provides a rare oppor-tunity to experience what the ancient Maltese people might have experienced at this temple at that time. Of course, we don't know how they celebrated these events. Did they dance and drum? Was there elaborate ceremony inside and/or outside? Perhaps crowds waited in the large forecourt but only a limited number entered the temple. After all, it is not a large interior space, and 20–30 people are sufficient to line the sides of the corridor leading to the altar.

Our experience at Mnajdra

Elyn's experience: The first time I came to Mnajdra, I felt like a tuning fork being struck. And that was just on a normal, as-tronomically non-significant day. So I eagerly looked forward to seeing the spring-equinox sun rise and shine its light into the Lower Temple. I wanted to experience something faintly like the ancient Maltese might have experienced at this sacred site at this powerful, momentarily-in-equilibrium time of year. I imagined a peaceful, centered group of participants, greeting the rising sun with respect and gratitude.

It is never good to have expectations.

In the chilly March morning, in the dim light of just-before-dawn, a diverse group of 25 people followed the Heritage Malta guide down the long walkway to Mnajdra Temples. He gath-ered us around him in the forecourt and began to drone on and on about the history and significance of the place and the event. He seemed determined to keep people from performing any act that might be considered "spiritual"—including greeting the sunrise in silence.

Surreptitiously, I wandered away and entered the temple. The first time I was there, I had been able to walk up to the altar at the rear. Now it was roped off. Disappointed, I sat on a low, pitted stone in the first apse and entered into stillness. Soon a few other women joined me, eager to conduct their own, semi-private ritual before anyone else—even the rising sun—entered into the sacred space.

After what seemed like much-too-long after sunrise—I had forgotten that the sun had to rise above the eastern hills—a faint glimmer of light began to penetrate the temple's central axis. Soon the passageway was lined two-deep with chattering people taking selfies as the ray of sunlight lit up the stone altar at the rear of the temple.

We had participated in an event that had first been honored in this powerful place over 5,000 years ago. I was sure that we had not witnessed it in the way the ancient Maltese had—but, in fact, I don't know how they would have celebrated the equinox sunrise. Perhaps they would have been equally animated—but without cellphones.

Gary's Experience: I used my dowsing rods to find energy lines as we walked to Mnajdra, and I found seven "gateways," locations where my rods suddenly rotated. The eighth gateway was at the snake threshold at the South Temple. I think of these gateways as concentric rings of protective energy, still active millennia after the temples were in active use. I have found these many times before at sacred sites, including in Brittany, Ireland, and Wales, though the number of gateways varies depending on the location. These "circles of protection" can be felt if you walk slowly and with intention. Pause at each one and ask permission to continue.

Entry Information

Both Ħaġar Qim and Mnajdra are managed by Heritage Malta. See http://heritagemalta.org. The Heritage Malta Multisite Pass allows entry to both.

A limited number of tickets are available for advance purchase online for Heritage Malta-sponsored equinox and solstice events at Mnajdra and Ħaġar Qim. The events at Mnajdra are scheduled for two days, four times a year—the spring and autumn equinoxes and the summer and winter solstices. The events at Ħaġar Qim are only scheduled during the summer and winter solstices. For each day, there are 40 tickets available for Mnajdra and 10 for Ħaġar Qim. Access is strictly controlled and includes a guide who explains in detail about the temples and their orientations. The ticket includes free time to explore Mnajdra and Ħaġar Qim and access to the Visitor Center.

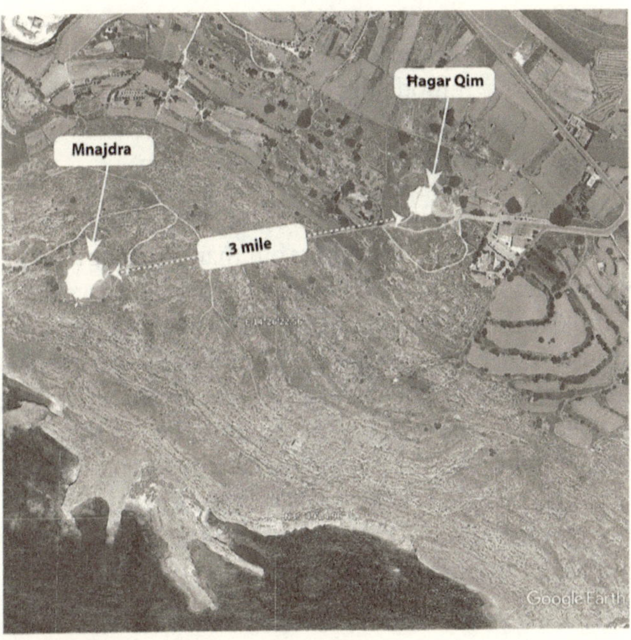

Getting There

Ħaġar Qim and Mnajdra are 1.25 miles southwest of Qrendi in southwest Malta. Regular buses from Valletta and both "Hop On Hop Off" bus services (City Sight Seeing South Route and Malta Sightseeing South/Red Tour) stop near the Visitor Center. Taxis will take you there early in the morning.

Controversies

Although there is no doubt that astronomical events are important at these temples, there is some disagreement about which ones.

Ħaġar Qim

Heritage Malta schedules summer and winter sunrise solstice events at Ħaġar Qim. Special entry is permitted with advanced reservation and purchase of an additional ticket.

Klaus Albrecht says that Ħaġar Qim is built with different axes relating to the various positions of the sun.[71] Because of the extensive remodeling of the Main Temple, he found it difficult to determine whether they were intentionally linked to astronomical events.

Lenie Reedijk bases her analysis of Ħaġar Qim on the precession of the star Sirius. She points out that, "The ideal location from which to watch this delightful phenomenon was a point on a hill by the coast, allowing an unobstructed view of the southern horizon across the sea."[72] In other words: at Ħaġar Qim. According to her calculations, the small, older temple called Ħaġar Qim North was oriented to the setting of Sirius around 9150 BCE. This would make that temple the oldest (surviving) temple on Malta. Ħaġar Qim Main, on the other hand, was built much later and was oriented toward the rising of Sirius around 4650 BCE.

Mnajdra

It has been suggested that Mnajdra South (Lower) Temple was oriented toward "the heliacal rise of the Pleiades rather than towards equinox sunrise" and that the lines of drilled holes in Mnajdra East recorded the risings of stars, "starting with the Pleiades."[73] However, most researchers agree that Mnajdra South (Lower) Temple is oriented to the spring and autumn equinoxes. And, thanks to the developing field of archaeo-astronomy, there is little doubt that this temple is also designed to mark the summer and winter solstices and the cross-quarter days (February 1, May 1, August 1, and November 1).

Klaus Albrecht set up his tripod in the northern (Central) Temple at Mnajdra to watch the Winter Solstice Sunrise.[74] He was not disappointed. In fact, he observed the sunrise coming in the main entrance. Soon, light illuminated the left altar stone and brought a play of shadow and light to the small graffito of the temple on the orthostat. He also recorded the sunbeams hitting the upright stones on the right and left of the central passage at Mnajdra South.

Lenie Reedijk believes that Mnajdra North was oriented to the setting of Sirius around 7950 BCE, Mnajdra Central to the rising of Sirius around 6150 BCE, and Mnajdra South was, as we have seen, oriented to solar rather than stellar events. In fact, "These discoveries at Mnajdra South established the proof...that the ancient Maltese were highly interested in celestial phenomena..."[75] And, as Reedijk points out, that includes stellar events as well as solar.

Tore Lomsdalen's detailed and careful archaeo-astronomy examination of Mnajdra has led him to propose the following chronology. Mnajdra East was probably the first temple and was constructed from 3600–3000 BCE. Mnajdra North could have been built in the middle and later Tarxien Phase (3000–2500 BCE), starting with the back apses. Mnajdra South could have been constructed in four stages, with part of it as old or older than Mnajdra East. He believes it was constructed and altered over a period of at least 1000 years.[76]

The Temples: More Controversies

Now that we have briefly "visited" a number of temples and caves on Malta, let's revisit some of the questions we asked in the introduction.

Three Inter-related Questions about the Maltese Temples

Why did the master builders construct so many temples, and why were some temples constructed either next to or intruding into each other? And the third question: how old are the temples, really?

Let's begin by acknowledging that there is probably no way of knowing the answers to these questions. But this doesn't stop people—including us—from coming up with more or less convincing, and often conflicting, solutions. Remember: "Everybody has an agenda" and unconscious biases.

Why so many temples?

One survey indicates 66 prehistoric temples were constructed on Malta. The archaeological consensus is that they were constructed over a period of at least 1500 years. Hence, a number of them may have been in use at the same time.

Constructing this many megalithic temples on Malta was not an easy project, no matter how skilled the builders. They only had wood, stone, leather, and antlers with which to quarry rock and sculpt stone. They had no wheeled vehicles that we know of, no metal, no heavy-duty construction machinery with which to transport and erect massive stones, some weighing as much as 20 tons. There must have been an important reason—or several—for ancient Maltese farmers to dedicate so much difficult, time-consuming effort to building multiple sacred sites over the centuries.

Perhaps the ancient Maltese built so many temples so that they wouldn't have to walk far to reach one. Or perhaps they built them as a demonstration of community solidarity or, perhaps, community rivalry. Or maybe the numerous temples are an indication of a developing priesthood (male or female) that required new building projects to assert or to enhance its prestige and power.

A very different explanation is suggested by those who believe Malta was the original Atlantis. They believe that when Atlantis sank beneath the seas during an environmental cataclysm, it left behind the "mountaintops" that make up Malta as we see it today.[77] There is indeed evidence that Malta once formed a land bridge to Sicily and to North Africa. This land bridge was submerged at the end of the last Ice Age, leaving above water what is now known as the Maltese archipelago. The rising Mediterranean, along with earthquakes, faulting, and subsidence, created the Malta we see today.

This doesn't mean Malta was Atlantis, but if Malta were Atlantis, it would have been a very important cultural and religious center for a wide area. This could explain why there were so many temples—including, perhaps, others that are submerged beneath the waters. There are reports that the remains of one such temple were still visible in Valletta Harbor in the early 19th century.[78]

Another explanation is that not only was Malta Atlantis, it was chosen to be Atlantis by Star Beings from Sirius. According to Francis Aloisio, "Malta's role was to receive the first Star Seed and to be the hub for anchoring Cosmic Energy and Starlight on Earth."[79] During the Paleolithic era, the Star Queen chose Malta for a very special mission. These Star Beings built the temples to fulfill that mission.

According to Aloisio's understanding, Gozo was chosen as the "nerve center" and administrative seat for the King and Queen of Atlantis[80]; Malta was chosen as the power generator, educational center, and industrial area.[81] "Thus the main purpose of the temples was to generate 'life' and to draw the power of the heavens into the womb of the earth, and to transmit it to the other power stations around the world through the electromagnetic grid in order to energize and vitalize the planet."[82] Each temple had and still has a particular purpose, and they are "5D-Consciousness, expressed, presented and shaped in 3D-Form."[83]

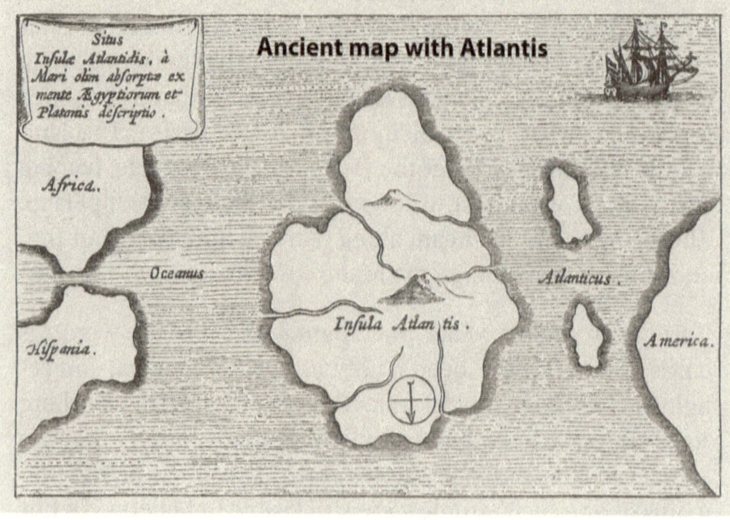

There is yet another possibility. As we have seen, Lenie Reedijk proposes that the reason there are so many temples on Malta is that they were built sequentially to be in alignment with the gradually changing rising (or setting) location of the star Sirius.[84] As the rising and setting point of Sirius gradually "drifted" out of alignment with the orientation of the central axis of a specific temple, a new temple was constructed with a slightly different alignment. Her theory requires that the temples were built not over a period of 1500 years but over a period of at least 5000 years, from 9150–4150 BCE, making them much older than the archaeologically agreed-upon time frame. Why was Sirius so important? We don't know.

Let's turn the question around and look at it from a different perspective. Is it really so unusual to have numerous temples in a relatively small landmass? Today nearly every Maltese village has its own church, making a combined total of 359 on Malta and Gozo. These churches, often within sight of each other, are seen as an example of religious fervor and an expression of village pride and competition. We can't know what the ancient Maltese were thinking about or trying to express with their numerous temples, but the presence of so many places of worship coexisting at the same time, for whatever reasons, is not unheard of—and may be not so unusual.

Why were some of the temples built so close together or, sometimes, intruding into each other?

None of the researchers we have consulted has a theory about why the temples are constructed in such close proximity to each other. None except Lenie Reedijk. Her detailed analyses of Ġgantija, Tarxien, and Mnajdra provide an intriguing explanation for why some of these temples were built so close together—even requiring modification of the earlier building(s) and perimeter walls at the sites so that they could "share" the same space. It all has to do with the gradual precession of Sirius and the need to build new temples with different orientations. Her analysis concludes that the temples were constructed in a very different order, from the smallest and simplest temple—Ħaġar Qim North—to the largest and much more complex Ġgantija South.

A different hypothesis (which doesn't negate Reedijk's) is that the temples were constructed in close proximity to each other because the specific location was powerful. After all, the original temple had been in use for centuries before the subsequent temple was built, so the land was sanctified—as was the building. In addition, there may be telluric energies (underground water lines or fault lines, energy vortices, etc.) that enhance the energy of buildings erected on that location. Or perhaps available land was in short supply.

Maybe the master builders constructed temples that encroached on earlier ones because it was more efficient to remodel and/or expand an existing building than to start over in a different location. For comparison, we can look at the way many medieval Christian sacred sites have been altered over the centuries. Rather than erecting a new cathedral or church, builders often expanded the existing one, changing its floorplan and exterior dimensions to give it an "upgrade."

Reedijk's calculations about the precession of Sirius are complex and thorough, and if she is correct, they require a complete reorganization of the chronology of the Maltese temples. However, her theory does not explain why the subsequent temples do not appear to have been built at regular time intervals. A standard time interval of approximately 200 years would make sense, given the gradual precessional shift of Sirius.

Nor does her theory explain why the subsequent temple was often built in a completely different location on the islands from the previous temple in the sequence. One could hypothesize that an underlying egalitarianism required the builders to spread the temples throughout Malta and Gozo, eventually returning to a previous location to construct another one. Perhaps there was something like a lottery. Or perhaps the choice of location reflected shifting political power centers or tribal or clan dynamics (if they had those types of social organization). Too many temples and too much evidence have been destroyed for Reedijk to be able to adequately address these questions.

How old are the temples, really?

So far we have seen several different timelines for the temples. The archaeological timeline estimates the Temple Period ranges from 4000 BCE (at the very earliest) to 2350 BCE (at the very latest). Reedijk's hypothesis states that Ħaġar Qim North was the first temple and was built in 9150 BCE to align with the setting of Sirius.

Francis Aloisio dismisses the idea that Neolithic farmers from Sicily built the temples. He thinks they were constructed much earlier by Star Beings. He points out that, although the early pottery at the sites is similar to that found on Sicily, that doesn't mean that people from Sicily built the temples—or that they built them at such a late date.[85]

Graham Hancock[86] and Anton Mifsud et al.[87] suggest that the temples are probably much older than we know and that earlier temples lie buried under the rising Mediterranean waters. Rather than suddenly being constructed without antecedents, the complex megalithic temples that we see were the result of a slow developmental process; we just haven't discovered the antecedents.

Hancock declares that "we are a culture with amnesia"[88] and suggests that an earlier civilization may have built the temples or at least contributed the necessary knowledge—an earlier civilization destroyed by the massive cataclysms at the start and end of the Younger Dryas (c. 10,800–9700 BCE). Recent excavations at the Anatolian site Göbekli Tepe have uncovered for the first time impressive free-standing monuments that date to exactly that time frame.

Expanding on Hancock's perspective, Freddy Silva writes in his recent book, "As with Egypt, the Maltese temples may be vestiges of a lost antediluvian civilization, after all, sites that once stood on dry land now lie two miles offshore and under twenty-five feet of seawater."[89] He goes on to argue that

Malta's temples belong "to a remote age, say, 14,000 years ago."[90] This would require human settlement on Malta before the last Ice Age—a controversial topic we discussed earlier in relationship to Għar Dalam and Għar Hasan (see p. 24).

Silva notes that 14,000 years ago, the alignments of Ġgantija North would have matched the spring equinox sunrise, and the entrance at Ġgantija South would have marked the Major Lunar Standstill. Silva would agree that the temples were in use during much later times, but he argues that later use doesn't tell us when they were first built. And that the first temples built were constructed with much more technical expertise than the later ones.

If this theory is correct, then one can understand how the largest temples—Ġgantija Temples—would have been the earliest. Over millennia, the knowledge that had been handed down from the antediluvian civilization was gradually lost, so more recent temples were less well constructed and smaller. However, counter to that argument, most archaeologists consider Tarxien Temples the most advanced in terms of workmanship, and archaeologists generally agree that these are more recent than Ġgantija.

Reedijk's timeline suggests that the master builders became more, not less, skilled, and that the biggest temple (Ġgantija South) is the most recent and small Ħaġar Qim North Temple is the oldest. In her theory, Ġgantija South Temple dates to 4250 BCE, not 12,000 BCE, as Silva would suggest.

Unfortunately, there is a paucity of verified dating for the temples—and for much else that has been discovered on Malta. Much vital evidence has been disturbed because of the inexorable passage of time and rampant urban development. Perhaps new data will come to light or new dating methods will be developed. Or, perhaps, we will never know.

Astronomical Alignments and the Temples

Although the first speculations about the connection between the Maltese temples and the sky were made in 1840 by J. G. Vance, researchers ignored the possibilities.[91] In 1934, the archaeologist Luigi Ugolini investigated Maltese temples and concluded that there was indeed some "connection between the central axes of the temples and the motion of the stars or other objects we see in the sky."[92] His findings were also ignored.

As late as 2008, archaeologist David Trump stated categorically, "Clearly the builders saw some significance in their alignments, though unrelated to the movements of the heavenly bodies."[93] This is a surprising comment since ancient people depended for their survival on knowledge of the annual seasonal cycle. Hunters needed to know when the herds would start to migrate. Farmers required detailed awareness of the annual solar cycle to know when to plant, when to harvest, when longer days and shorter nights will return, and when the rainy season should arrive. Communities needed to know when their rites, rituals, and festivals would occur.

Several artifacts other than temple alignments affirm that the ancient master builders did indeed look to the sky. We have already mentioned the so-called "sun sherd" found at Ħaġar Qim, which seems to show a solar wheel divided into eight sections.[94] Perhaps this is a reference to the cross-quarter days marked at nearby Mnajdra South Temple.

An 11.5" stone slab from Tal-Qadi Temple in northern Malta is engraved with a crescent and 24 asterisks, divided into pie-wedge sectors. It seems likely that these represent a crescent moon and stars, although we don't know what the significance is.[95] Another possible indication of stellar tracking is the orthostat with lines of pecked dots found in Mnajdra East Temple, which may have been used to track the rising of the Pleiades.[96]

Many Neolithic people kept detailed track of the sun and of the cycles of the moon. For example, Callanish Stone Circle on the Isle of Lewis, Scotland, constructed about 2900 BCE, marks the 18.6 year cycle of the major lunar standstill. That iconic English site Stonehenge, built at least by 3000 BCE, is believed to mark not only the solstices but also events such as the lunar standstill. Lomsdalen suggests that Mnajdra North Temple also marked the lunar standstill. Ancient, non-literate people didn't keep track of these cycles in writing; instead, they recorded them using the placement of stones.

We might ask how these ancient people could measure and keep track of these time spans—but that is an entirely different question than did they.[97]

In recent years, archaeo-astronomists have demonstrated that numerous ancient sites all over the world were built with a highly sophisticated awareness of different solar and celestial events, though exactly which events can sometimes be difficult to sort out. Without having been there when these monuments were constructed, there are some things we cannot know.

Let's look again at some of the Maltese temples. The first thorough survey of the orientations of the temples was done in the winter of 1979–1980 by George Agius and Frank Ventura.[98] Their data, based on measurements of 20 central corridor axes and 6 side entrance axes, showed that "the builders had preferred to set the entrances to face a direction between southeast and southwest."[99] It was analyzing this data that led Reedijk to her conclusions about the precession of Sirius.

Of all the temples on Malta, only Mnajdra South is oriented due east and west. That this alignment marks the sunrise at various times of the year is indisputable. We could say that Mnajdra South was designed as a solar temple. Or, more cautiously, we could say that Mnajdra South is aligned east-west and faces the rising equinoctial sunrise, and that this required precise measurements and was not accidental. In addition, various orthostats in Mnajdra South were erected in careful relationship to the entrance in order to mark the solstices and the cross-quarter days. Tore Lomsdalen's painstaking fieldwork has affirmed this.[100]

Acknowledging these alignments does not mean that we can say the ancient Maltese worshipped the sun or the moon, or Sirius, or the Pleiades. It does mean that the master builders considered the repetitive pattern important—important enough to construct a temple aligned in such a way that it would, like a calendar, mark a number of cyclical astronomical occurrences.

Several of the authors we have consulted have very different ideas about what the ancient temple builders were looking at in the heavens. Freddy Silva thinks one temple was oriented to the major lunar standstill and another to the summer solstice.[101] Lenie Reedijk thinks the master builders were looking at the rising and setting of Sirius.[102] Klaus Albrecht believes that most of the temples show some kind of solar alignment.[103] And Tore Lomsdalen suggests a nuanced and varied set of alignments at different temples.[104]

With modern computer technology, it is easy to "data-mine" and find some celestial event that matches some opening or alignment (axis, doorway, oracle hole, etc.) in a temple. Unless the celestial event is unequivocal, it is important to search for supportive evidence and evaluate it from a number of perspectives. In some cases, it is impossible to know whether a solar or stellar orientation is circumstantial, accidental, or intentional. But this doesn't mean that all astronomical associations are doubtful—nor that the ancient Maltese had no interest in recording the changes they saw every night in the star-filled sky.

The Presence of the Earth/Mother Goddess in Statues and Temple Layouts

We approach this topic with some trepidation. Ever since Marija Gimbutas' groundbreaking work in the 1970s, Malta has been considered the Land of the Goddess.[105] Without doubt, Gimbutas' work was a major corrective to a predominantly patriarchal reading of ancient history. It appears, however, that in some cases she may have overstated her argument.[106]

The statues

Let's begin exploring the presence of the Goddess on Malta by looking at the statues. A number of stone or clay human-like representations have been found in the temples, many of which we have described already. Some of them are unequivocally female: the Venus of Ħaġar Qim, the crude pregnant-lady statuettes found in Mnajdra and Tarxien, and the exquisite Sleeping Lady discovered in a pit in Ħal Saflieni Hypogeum. They have breasts and, in some cases, swollen bellies. Other female representations have been found as well, including a fragmented clay figure from Skorba, dating approximately 4400–4100 BCE. This crude, 3.5" high statuette appears to have a featureless head, plump breasts, and wide hips.

No unequivocally male statues have been found, though it has been proposed that the Tarxien terracotta statue with a solemn expression and long skirt/kilt is possibly a representation of a priest. There are, however, limestone carvings found at Tarxien that represent phalli.

Malta is famous for what are called "Fat Lady" statues. We have intentionally referred to them as obese statues in order to not pre-judge their gender. These statues are unique to Malta and are found in numerous temples and in a variety of sizes. The largest is the incomplete lower half of the 9' high stone statue found in the first apse on the right at Tarxien. Others are much smaller—only 3" high. Some are standing and others sitting.

These statues vary in some details, but, in general, they are characterized by huge hips and thighs, ballooning calves, and tiny feet. They have ample waists and, often, inflated arms as well. Often the arms are crossed over the waist or lower belly, though sometimes the right arm points down. They wear a short, medium, or long skirt (or kilt) and nothing on their upper torso. Some have small heads with indications of various hairdos; many do not have heads, either because they were removable or because they have been broken off. Many of them lack corresponding depth from front to back: in other words, the emphasis is placed on their ampleness as seen from the front.

Although a few of these obese figures have noticeable breasts or at least some indication of breasts, by far the majority of them do not. Some have flat chests without any kind of sculptured detail; others have a line or lines on their upper torsos that might indicate a horizontal fold, or a double arch, or a disk, or some kind of padding.

Many museum labels and guidebooks refer to these figures as "Fat Ladies" (or goddesses). We were puzzled by this. To us, they looked obese but not particularly female. Then we realized that if you call their clothing a skirt, rather than a kilt, you are predisposed to assume the figures are female. We also realized that there is a presumption that corpulence is a female attribute. But Mediterranean and North African (and Turkish) men also have a tendency to become plump—as did eunuchs, but that was due to hormonal imbalances resulting from castration.

We believe that if you were to see these figurines without any previous information, you would probably state that some are female and many are genderless, perhaps androgynous, possibly male, although they don't have any distinguishing masculine features. You would not think that they all represented women—especially the ones that don't have breasts.

When we asked a Goddess-celebrating friend about these amply proportioned statues, she asserted that of course they were Goddess figures, and that their lack of breasts was irrelevant. We said that seemed surprising, given the importance of breasts in the widespread "Venus" figures, including the Venus of Ħaġar Qim. She replied that breasts must simply not have been a significant iconographic feature for the ancient Maltese. Maybe this is true. But if so, why do some of the statues have breasts and others not?

We are willing to consider that our Goddess-celebrating friend may be more in touch with the intended meaning of these figures than we are. She has an intuitive connection with the Mother/Earth Goddess, whose presence she strongly felt on Malta. But she can't really know how or what the ancient Maltese worshipped.

As early as 1912, the Egyptologist T. Eric Peet identified the figures as female and labeled them as steatopygous.[107][108] Steatopygia describes a condition, usually found in tropical regions, of large accumulations of subcutaneous fat in the buttocks. It can occur even when the fat layer in the rest of the body is moderate. It usually occurs in women but can occur in males, and often among certain specific African communities.

One researcher asserts, "...it seems that steatopygia has been a beauty idea in some indigenous societies. From an evolutionary perspective, steatopygia helps people survive periods of severe food shortage."[109]

There are significant problems with deciding that the Maltese obese figurines are female because they have steatopygia. First, there is no evidence that the ancient Maltese had this condition. Second, the figurines are voluminous all over their bodies—including calves, torsos, and, often, arms. This is not what steatopygia looks like. It is, however, what lipidoema (the "bilateral, symmetrical enlargement of the buttocks and lower limbs owing to excess deposition of subcutaneous fat") can look like.

In lipidoema's most severe form, the lower half of the body is excessively large—with balloon-like buttocks, thighs, and swollen, sausage-like calves. The excessive fat deposits stop at the ankles, however, leaving what appear to be disproportionately small feet unaffected by the disorder. The trunk and arms can also be affected. While steatopygia may have some evolutionary advantages, lipidoema can be a painful and severely disabling condition. It occurs in women and almost never in men.

We are not suggesting that Maltese artists were trying to represent steatopygia or lipidoema in their obese statues. That would be making yet another mistake: assuming that an artistic representation is literal rather than symbolic.

David Trump stated in 1972 that "to describe [the large statue fragment at Tarxien] as a goddess or 'fat lady' may be no more than male prejudice. The sex [gender] is not explicitly indicated."[110] However, by 2008 he had changed his mind and called it female, probably a Mother Goddess[111]—while at the same time he still acknowledged that to call the statue a "fat lady" is "not actually borne out by the evidence. However, there is even less to suggest a male attribution."[112] Trump does point out that "absence of vulva or breasts on most of the ['fat lady'] statues is strange if fertility was the underlying principle of their religion." Indeed.

If they are not female, or if nurture and fertility are not their central motif, what might they represent? Maybe these figures are intended to epitomize abundance and prosperity, represented by a genderless, corpulent being. Such an image emphasizes bountiful food supplies rather than nurture and fertility, so breasts might not have been so important. Perhaps the headless statues would have had either male or female heads inserted into them, depending on the ritual occasion. If so, the Maltese have something to teach us about gender fluidity and our own modern Western assumptions about what people should look like.

The goddess in the temples

We have frequently read that the temples, like the unique obese statues, represent the Goddess. Cheryl Straffon says, "It is well known that the temples were deliberately shaped to form the body of a woman, or as a living reflection of the Goddess. This can be seen most clearly in Ġgantija on Gozo where the South Temple in particular has the characteristic 5 apse. This anthropomorphic temple is the oldest one to be dated: the top part was built around 3600 BCE."[113]

David Trump acknowledges, "There is an undoubted resemblance in outline between the plans of some of the temples and the seated 'fat lady' figurines. Is this coincidence or was one influenced by the other?" However, he continues, "it is only one form of the statuettes, the seated ones, and one of the temples, that with four apses and niche, where the similarity occurs at all. Regretfully, any relationship between the two, beyond the fact that both served the same religion, must be considered unlikely."[114]

There is no doubt that the Maltese temple shape—perimeter walls enclosing 3, 4, 5, or 6 ovoid apses—is unique. Rounded, curvaceous—it's easy to see why someone might think the 4- and 5-apse temples mimic the "Fat Lady" statues and, hence, the Goddess. Maybe they do. However, we have already pointed out that the corpulent statues may not all be female. If the rotund figures aren't all female, how can the temples, based on that shape, represent the body of the Goddess?

Although Trump considers it unlikely, it would not be surprising, in fact, if the shape of many of the temples has a relationship with the ancient Maltese image of the Divine. As Trump observes, "both [temples and statuettes] served the same religion...." Cruciform Christian churches architecturally recall the crucifix. For many Christians, entering into a church is like symbolically entering into the body of Christ, whose heart is "located" at the crossing and whose head is at the altar.[115] It's probable that the ancient Maltese master builders were expressing a similar understanding: sacred space represented their concept of the Divine.

From what we think we know about the ancient Maltese, they belonged to a peaceful and cooperative society, without a marked hierarchy or class structure. They were quite skilled and knew how to build massive stone buildings and orient them to complex astronomical events. We don't know what their religion was, but we see in their artwork flowing, organic forms, some animal representations, and precise spiral designs. We see in their statuary female figurines, male phalli, androgynous statuettes, and several examples of snakes.

Perhaps what the curvaceous temples and the obese statues show us is that a culture doesn't have to emphasize the masculine over the feminine—or vice versa. Instead, it can find and maintain a harmonious, inclusive balance—a balance that appears to have lasted for at least 1500 years.

The Cart-Ruts

Malta is a puzzling, enigmatic land, and the so-called "cart-ruts" are one more baffling example of why this is true. The label "cart-rut," like the label "Fat Lady" statue, only adds to the confusion. Although nobody really knows what they are, they do not seem to have been cart-ruts.

Malta's limestone plateaus are crisscrossed by numerous paired ruts that turn, twist, cross, and go up and down the side of hills. Some even go under water and resurface miles away on the island of Filfla, off the southern coast of Malta. Although cart-ruts are found in other countries, and more modern cart-ruts are found on Malta, they differ in a number of respects from the earliest Maltese cart-ruts.

The cart-ruts occur all over Malta and Gozo.[116] Many have been destroyed by building projects or are buried under profuse plant growth. Some of the best-preserved on the island of Malta are found at Clapham Junction, named after the south London railway hub, located south of Mdina/Rabat, south of Buskett Gardens; at San Pawl Tat-Targa, in the limits of Naxxar; and at Dingli Cliffs. At St. George's Bay, Birżebbuġa, Malta, cart-ruts go under the water. There are fewer cart-ruts on Gozo, but notable ones can be seen at Dwejra and Ta' Ċenċ Cliffs.

They always occur in pairs, hence the name cart-ruts. They are V-shaped, with narrow grooves and a rounded bottom. They vary in depth from 18" to 24". Sometimes the same pair of ruts changes dramatically in depth, becoming quite shallow and even disappearing, and sometimes one rut in a pair is deeper than the other. They differ in length from relatively short to over a mile.

The gauge (the distance between the paired ruts) is more or less uniform. On the average, it is 4.6', about the distance between modern railways tracks. However, the gauge of an individual pair can vary by an inch at different points along its length. This would have made it impossible for a cart with a fixed-wheel axis to use the cart-ruts. In the raised limestone between the paired ruts, there is no indication of wear caused by animal hooves or human feet.

Sometimes only a few cart-ruts are found wending their way across the limestone plateaus. At other times they occur in a dense profusion, overlapping and crossing each other at various angles, and then heading off in different directions. Clapham Junction is the best example of this bewildering complexity.

We don't know how old the cart-ruts are, why they were constructed, how they were constructed, or how they were used. Theories proliferate, but all of them have their drawbacks. As David Trump writes, "[The cart-ruts have] many aspects, several of them still completely baffling, which of course adds greatly to their appeal. ... Definitive solutions seem as far off as ever."[117]

Dates ranging from the Neolithic Temple Period to the 16th century have been suggested. The Bronze Age and Classic periods are often favored, with the Phoenician era most popular, but nobody knows. Some of the cart-ruts lead down to the sea and are now covered by water, indicative of great age—but nobody knows how old. Others end abruptly at the edge of a cliff. Presumably, the rest of the cliff fell into the sea at some unknown time.

Several researchers associate the cart-ruts with quarries and construct a convincing story that some kind of vehicle was used to transport limestone blocks to build temples.[118] However, according to Trump, very few of the cart-ruts are actually associated with quarries—and none have been found to run to the megalithic Maltese temples.[119] He asserts, "Unfortunately, they all die out before reaching a clear destination."[120]

There is also the question of what kind of transport was used, if, indeed, the cart-ruts were used for transport. Researchers do not believe the ancient Maltese temple builders had the wheel. And even if they had wheeled carts—or the cart-ruts were made by later, Bronze-Age settlers who had the wheel—how could wheeled carts have functioned within the varied-width, very deep, and sometimes sharply turning cart-ruts? The short answer is: they couldn't.

Several other vehicles have been suggested, including a sledge with fixed runners (similar objections) and a slide car, similar to a North American travois. Instead of wheels or fixed runners, two long pieces of wood would have been fastened at one end to a powerful animal, such as an ox or horse. The lower ends would have dragged along the ground, eventually creating the cart-ruts. Whatever was being transported would have been placed on a platform between the two "slides."

A modern oxcart

The short answer to this scenario is that it also wouldn't have worked. Some of the cart-ruts are quite steep—briefly heading downhill (or uphill) at a 45° angle. This, and the tight curving turns of some of the cart-ruts, would have been very difficult to negotiate with an oxen-pulled slide car or a wheeled cart.

Another question is how were the cart-ruts made? That also is unclear. Were they naturally worn into the limestone, or were they the result of tedious excavation? Perhaps some unidentified object—a set of runners with a stone attached at the lower end, for example—began the process of wearing down the top soil and cutting into the underlying limestone. Trump is sure that, however they were started, they were worn down with use.

Recent geomorphology research examined the material properties and erosion processes associated with the cart-ruts.[121] The geologists demonstrated that if a heavy weight is pulled over wet limestone, the limestone wears down surprisingly quickly. But this still doesn't explain what vehicle was used or what it carried. And although Malta has a rainy season, it is also quite arid.

What were they used for? For the purpose of discussion, let's assume that some unspecified type of vehicle was used that carried something heavy, and it did so frequently and over a long period of time. Immediately one thinks of transporting from quarries the large limestone blocks used to build the megalithic temples. We have already seen that although some researchers find a correlation between the temples and quarries, Trump rejects their conclusions. Several cart-ruts can be shown, however, to run to fortified Bronze Age villages, but Trump considers that evidence circumstantial and not sufficient.

Some people theorize that the cart-ruts were used for irrigation purposes, but they do not appear to be related to water sources—or if so, only rarely—nor is it clear how the water would have been transported. Perhaps some kind of vehicle used the ruts to carry produce and fishing catch from one place to another, but such relatively light goods seem unlikely to have created such deep cart-ruts. And why so many?

Antonio Arnaiz-Villena et al. make a novel proposal, based on comparisons between Maltese cart-ruts and those on the Canary Islands. "In other words, cart-ruts may have been used to measure time and space direction (astronomy/geography). Shadows made by hills or sticks on cart-ruts may have measured Sun and other astronomical parameters."[122] They think the cart-ruts date to the Bronze Age, and they also suggest that the cart-ruts could have been used for different purposes at different times and in different locations.

Given all the confusion about the cart-ruts, perhaps Trump has the best way to approach them. He says, "There can be few activities as stimulating as the pursuit of cart-ruts. On the one hand, tracing them across the Maltese countryside, watching for every little detail as to where they run next and admiring the wild flowers on the way, is surely as rewarding a physical exercise as any. ... There is then the mental exercise of trying to make sense of them. ... Malta's cart-ruts would be much less exciting if we knew all the answers."[123]

Getting There

Buses go to several towns that have cart-ruts nearby. Regular buses run between Valletta (Malta) and Naxxar, and between Victoria (Gozo) and Ta' Ċenċ. Clapham Junction is approximately 2.5 miles south of Rabat (Malta). There is frequent bus service to Rabat from Valletta, but getting to Clapham Junction, south of Buskett Gardens, probably requires a car or taxi—or a long walk. From Rabat to Clapham Junction is 2.7–3.3 miles on foot, depending on the route.

Controversies

There is a lot of controversy with regard to the cart-ruts, some of which we have already described. Archaeologist Anthony Bonanno disagrees with archaeologist David Trump's assessment of their age (probably Bronze Age), his assertion that "only two cart-ruts terminate at a quarry," and his belief that the quarry may have been excavated after the cart-ruts rather than used in conjunction with them.

As a result of studies Bonanno has conducted over 40 years of his academic career, he is convinced that the cart-ruts are almost invariably associated with quarries. He points out that Clapham Junction "lies next to the largest and most important concentration of Malta's ancient quarries."[124] He believes they were used to transport stone building blocks, and he finds parallels in other locations in Europe.

Bonanno asserts that, most probably, the cart-ruts date to Phoenician, Punic, and Roman times.[125] As a result of a thorough survey undertaken by two of his students, he states unequivocally that "the outstanding majority (exceeding 80%) of cart-ruts are clearly associated with quarries of the Classical age...."[126] In contrast, many fewer cart-ruts appear to be associated with Bronze Age sites.

The archaeologist Claudia Sagona believes that instead of ruts worn by carts, the cart-ruts are field-furrow scars.[127] She uses this hypothesis as evidence for support of her theory of strategies for ancient field production in the Late Neolithic.

If these archaeologists are in such fundamental conflict on so many aspects of the cart-ruts, how can a lay reader possibly determine what they were used for—and, even, where they went?

Let's try a different approach. What happens if we don't call these parallel grooves "cart-ruts"? Numerous alternative explanations then arise.

For example, there are theories that the cart-ruts were used for some long-forgotten energy-generating technology, either derived from Atlantis or from visiting aliens. Francis Aloisio states that the Earth was struck by a passing meteorite, and the resulting orbital imbalance threatened to destroy the planet. "The temple builders [Star Beings from Sirius] pre-empted such a threat of the planet hurtling into space and destruction by building the ruts in Malta and the pyramid at Giza in Egypt. Thus, they managed to correct the disturbance in the geomagnetic field of the Planet and to re-balance its electromagnetic grids."[128]

Aloisio explains that the cart-ruts "were designed and built so that positive energy runs along one side of the parallel grooves while negative energy flows along the other side. They were moving a vast stream of consciousness and vital energy to all the temples around the island and the surrounding landmass through these invisible cable lines. This flow of electric energy kept everything in balance and healthy on Earth."[129] Because the Star Beings from Sirius couldn't explain the magnetic energy-field misalignment to the ancient Maltese and didn't want to panic them, the Star Beings "used some of these ruts for a practical purpose: to facilitate a mode of transport and to serve as water channels for irrigation."[130]

Another possibility is that the ruts were used for raising some kind of agricultural product. After all, for centuries, Maltese farmers have planted vines in holes they have dug in the limestone; they know that this helps shelter the roots from the arid summer heat. But this, too, seems unlikely.

Years ago, Erich von Däniken suggested that the Maltese labored "to cut stone signs in the ground in memory of or as homage to the extraterrestrials... ...To me, ruts, temples and Hypogeum are proof that 'gods' took a hand here."[131]

We leave it to you to come up with your own preferred explanation. Meantime, following the cart-ruts is a fine way to enjoy a day's outing on Malta.

Historical Sites and Places of Natural Beauty on Malta

A visitor to the islands can spend weeks exploring Roman villas, 16th century castle-forts, and WW II defensive sites, admiring the views from the vertiginous cliffs, relaxing in the sun on the long sandy beaches, diving in the crystal-blue sea, or just "chilling out" at a harbor-side fish restaurant. Standard travel guides describe these attractions in detail. Our focus in this book is on places we have found to be powerful, not just entertaining. The following section includes the historic sites and places of natural beauty that we have found to be very powerful.

The Island of Gozo

Calypso's Cave, north coast, Gozo — A mythical location

Not far from Ġgantija Temples and Xagħra Stone Circle is a cliff-side cave known by the evocative name of Calypso's Cave. The setting is spectacular, overlooking the reddish-gold sandy beach of Ramla Bay, Gozo's best beach for swimming, snorkeling, or simply "chilling out."

The cave itself has collapsed and is not accessible to visitors, but the overlook is well worth the visit. Reportedly, the cave itself was nothing much to see: a crevice under an overhang on the side of a cliff. Remains of a Roman bath or villa are hidden in the sand dunes below, along with fortifications, including a submerged wall in the bay, built by the Knights of Malta in the mid 18th century.

What makes this site powerful—aside from the view—is its possible association with Odysseus, hero of Homer's epic, *The Odyssey*. Homer composed the lengthy poem in the late 8th century BCE, probably recording stories that had been carried down by oral tradition. The part of the story that might concern Malta is as follows.

While returning home from the Trojan War, Odysseus's ship was blown off-course as punishment by the gods. All his companions drowned during the violent gales that created ship-tossing waves. He alone survived, and at last he washed up on the sandy shores of Ogygia (which was perhaps Gozo), the island home of Calypso, the daughter of the Titan Atlas. Calypso had been imprisoned on the island by the gods because she had supported her father in the battle between the Titans and Olympians.

Calypso Takes Pity on Odysseus

Calypso ensnared Odysseus with her enchanting singing while weaving at her loom with a golden shuttle. She wanted to keep him with her forever in her cave, and for a while he apparently was content. After all, she promised him eternal youth and immortality. But he yearned to return to Ithaca and to Penelope, his long-suffering, faithful wife. At last, after seven years, all-powerful Zeus forced Calypso to free Odysseus, and angrily Calypso agreed. Liberated at last, Odysseus set sail for home.

Although this is probably simply a legend, recounted in Homer's *Odyssey* as if it were an actual event, the story raises some interesting questions. The number 7 often has esoteric significance: 7 days in the week, 7 dwarfs, 7 heavens, 7 stars in the Pleiades, 7 planets known in ancient times, etc. Perhaps the legend is a distant and distorted recollection that something of importance occurred in this grotto. Perhaps the cave was the location of esoteric initiations, and only after 7 years of study was the apprentice considered qualified to be initiated. Or perhaps Odysseus represents the soul of the Seeker who, even while mired in sensual distractions, remembers its "true" home and longs for release.

Getting There

Calypso's Cave is located in the cliffs at the west end of Ramla Beach. Regular buses run frequently to the beach, and the overlook can be reached by hiking up a steep path. Numerous regular buses stop at Xagħra village square, and Calypso's Cave is a 30–40 minute walk from there, without requiring a climb up from the beach. Malta/Gozo Sightseeing "Hop On Hop Off" bus stops at Calypso Cave overlook. Gozo "Hop On Hop Off" T2 Route bus stops at Ramla, near Calypso's Cave.

The Inland Sea and Dwejra Cliffs, west coast, Gozo — Beauty surrounds us

Dwejra (dway-rah) has some spectacular scenery. Two vast limestone caverns collapsed eons ago, resulting in Dwejra Bay and the Inland Sea. The Inland Sea is a cliff-bound lagoon, used as a fishermen's base for centuries. A 110-yard-long tunnel-like opening through the cliffs connects the Inland Sea with Dwejra Bay.

The iconic Azure Window, a natural arch in the sea cliffs, used to draw even more tourists to this scenic spot. Unfortunately, the Azure Window collapsed in March 2017 from a combination of very bad weather and very slow erosion. Fortunately, nobody was injured.

Nearby Fungus Rock (AKA Mushroom Rock) guards the entrance to the Inland Sea. This looming, 197' high limestone rock was famous for the healing plant that grew on the rock's flat top during the time of the Knights of Malta. Misnamed *Fungus melitensis*, it is actually *Cynomorium coccineum*, a parasitic flowering plant with a repulsive fragrance. The plant acts as a styptic, stopping the flow of blood in wounds, which would have been very useful for the warrior knights. It also was used to treat diarrhea. The Knights gave samples of their closely guarded supply to their aristocratic friends.

In 1651, the Knights built Qawra Tower on the mainland across from the rock to defend their medicinal stock. Controlled access was provided by a precarious cable car from the mainland, 160' away. They also tried smoothing the rock's sides to remove handholds. Today, the rock is an off-limits nature preserve.

Short trips in small outboard-motorboats take tourists from the Inland Sea into the bay. The scenery is spectacular. The boat ride is a good way to see the limestone stratification in the sea-side cliffs and to admire the clear azure waters.

Our Experience at Dwejra

Elyn's Experience: Our "Hop On Hop Off" bus stopped at Dwejra, so we hopped off. I didn't expect much. In fact, I usually avoid hyped tourist destinations. Besides, I was worrying about whether we would have time to take the boat tour and return before the next bus arrived. I shouldn't have worried. And I shouldn't have hesitated. Our friendly fisherman-pilot waited until there were eight of us on board and then guided the boat from the Inland Sea, through the tunnel-like opening, into the bay. The views were stunning. He steered us close to the towering limestone cliffs, pointing out the orange color at the base of some of them and the intense blue of the crystalline sea. I was reminded that the most powerful place of all is Nature.

Getting There

Regular buses stop at Dwejra and at San Lawrenz, approx. 1 mile away. Gozo/Malta Sightseeing "Hop On Hop Off" bus stops at the Azure Window (Dwejra); Gozo City Sightseeing "Hop On Hop Off" buses stop at Dwejra. Several fishermen wait at the dock to provide 15-minute-long boat trips, timed to the arrival of the buses. The ride costs 4€/pp.

Ta' Pinu Basilica, near Gharb, northwest Gozo — A powerful pilgrimage shrine

This stunning church is Malta's National Shrine to the Virgin Mary. It is visible from a distance in the countryside near Gharb (aarb), its golden tower and dome standing out against the sky and sea. A short road leads to the basilica from the main highway. Five large commemorative frescoes extolling the many miracles of the Virgin Mary are erected along the sidewalk that flanks the road. This scenic walk prepares the pilgrims for their upcoming encounter with the sacred, and, indeed, it is called The Pilgrim's Way.

An expansive paved forecourt greets the visitor. In 2017, large canopied mosaics were mounted on semi-circular walls around the perimeter. They portray the 20 "Mysteries of the Rosary" and provide shade from the scorching summer sun.

If the forecourt isn't filled with people, you will notice a large, octagonal, dark grey-and-beige, 7-circuit labyrinth set into the pavement. A labyrinth is a design based on a single path that twists and turns in a repetitive pattern until it reaches the center.

This labyrinth is meant to be walked. There are many ways to walk a labyrinth, but we will suggest a simple practice to follow. Remember, this is not a maze with dead-ends and diversions that engage the mind like a puzzle. A labyrinth is a single path that leads into the center. It encourages a meditative mind-set.

Begin by being present to yourself and your surroundings. Pause, take a few breaths. Then set an intention or ask a question about something that is on your mind. Consider the possibility that whatever happens during your labyrinth walk will be meaningful for you. Be open to whatever calls your attention (a bird song? A breeze? A casual comment?).

Start walking the labyrinth. Notice the rhythmic pattern of the path you are following, moving toward and away from the center and back again. Perhaps someone else is walking with you. Notice how you walk together for a while, or how your paths diverge.

When you reach the center of the labyrinth, turn to face the four directions. The church, directly ahead of you, faces east. Then, focus on the directions "up" and "within." Pay attention to what you feel. Notice any insights that come to you. And then, walk out—but do so by following the labyrinth path in reverse, as if you are uncoiling a spring. This helps you to retain whatever new awareness you have gained on this mini-pilgrimage. When you reach the exit point, which was the entry point when you started, turn and give thanks for the experience, whatever it was.

Ta' Pinu basilica was built in a simple, neo-Romanesque architectural style between 1920 and 1931. It is shaped like the Latin cross, and it is decorated with beautiful statuary, six large mosaics, and 76 stained-glass windows, including Rose windows. The ornate, detached bell tower is 200' high and was built later.

The main altar is in the center, covered with a canopy or baldachin containing exquisite sculptures. Several rooms are lined with votive offerings—crutches, artificial limbs, baby clothes, radiation masks, plaster casts, ex-voto replicas of body parts, signed certificates, etc.—offered to "Our Lady of the Assumption" in hopes of, or in gratitude and thanksgiving for, miraculous cures.

The origin of Ta' Pinu church goes back centuries. The current church incorporates remains of a small 15th century (possibly older) church. The basilica takes its name from the caretaker of the old, decrepit church dedicated to Our Lady of the Assumption. His name was Filippino Gauci. "Pinu" is the diminutive for his first name. According to some reports, Filippino Gauci was made procurator of the old church in 1598 and later offered money for its restoration. Under his supervision, it was rebuilt but later fell once again into disrepair.

Some of the numerous ex-votos at Ta' Pinu Basilia

The story of the modern Ta' Pinu pilgrimage shrine begins with Carmela (Karmni) Grima, a deeply devoted woman. She used to say a prayer next to the run-down church before going back home after a day's hard work in the fields. She reported that in 1883, "Our Lady" (the Virgin Mary) spoke to her and told her, among other things, to recite specific prayers. Another local Maltese, Francis Portelli, reported around the same time that he heard the voice of the Virgin emanating from the 1619 painting of Our Lady of the Assumption inside the church.

Soon the Virgin of Ta' Pinu was reported to be working miracles. After lengthy investigation, the Church offered it official recognition, and pilgrimages began to be organized. The impressive modern church was built to replace the tiny original church. It was funded with the aid of donations from the faithful all over the world. Part of the original church, with Carmela Grima's tomb, was incorporated behind the altar in the Chapel of the Immaculate Conception, along with the tomb of Francis Portelli.

Across the road from the basilica, a track leads up Ghammer Hill to the Stations of the Cross. Also known as the Via Crucis or the Way of Sorrows, the path is lined with 14 marble statues, commemorating and retelling the story of Jesus' trial and subsequent crucifixion. Walking the Stations of the Cross is an important activity during the season of Lent, especially on Good Friday (the Friday before Easter).

Our Experience at Ta' Pinu

Elyn's Experience: Our "Hop On Hop Off" bus driver let us hop off where the road to Ta' Pinu meets the highway. As we walked along the sidewalk, we admired the golden-domed church standing out against the blue sky. When we reached the forecourt, we were surprised to see a large labyrinth laid into the pavement. We knew we had to begin our visit to the basilica by walking it. Soon two young children joined us, skipping across the labyrinth's path. I wondered if I should take this as a sign that I should be more playful and not so rigid in following the path I saw in front of me.

Soon the Mass ended, and visitors were briefly allowed to enter the church. I admit it: I didn't expect to feel anything. I hadn't felt anything in any of the other Maltese churches we had visited, so why here? But here was something completely different. Ta' Pinu was a place of great "juju." Overwhelmed, I sat down in an empty pew in front of the central altar. Soon I felt surrounded by stillness—and by limitless, compassionate, unconditional love. I had experienced my own kind of miracle.

Entry Information

Ta' Pinu is an active, functioning church. Baptisms take place there, along with regularly scheduled Masses. It's important to check the website for updates on the schedule and when visitors are allowed to enter. Check http://www.tapinu.org/ (in Maltese) or http://islandofgozo.org/place?id=239&item=ta%E2%80%99-pinu-sanctuary. There are strict requirements about modest attire, turning off cellphones, etc.

Getting There

Ta' Pinu is located 2 miles from the center of Gharb. Regular buses run to Gharb. Both "Hop On Hop Off" bus services stop at Ta' Pinu Sanctuary. If a stop at Ta' Pinu is not on the Gozo City Sightseeing T1 schedule, ask the bus driver if he will let you off at the road that leads to the basilica—and find out when and where he will return.

The Island of Malta

As befitting its millennia-long human occupation, Malta is full of impressive sites. We will mention a few that we have found to be surprisingly powerful.

St. John's Co-Cathedral, Valletta, Malta — The epitome of bling

St. John's Co-Cathedral is an over-the-top paean to conspicuous consumption. It is a co-cathedral because, since 1816, it has shared cathedral status with St. Paul's Cathedral in Mdina, the official seat of the Archbishop of Malta. It is dedicated to St. John the Baptist, the patron saint of the Knights of St. John (AKA the Knights of Malta; originally known as the Knights Hospitaller).

St. John's Co-Cathedral has been called "a most glorious and magnificent artistic expression of the High Baroque era." The Knights of St. John arrived on Malta in 1530 and by 1577 had completed building this church. A century later, the interior was exuberantly remodeled into a flamboyant display of marble columns, twining flowers and garlands and angels carved into gold-leaf-encrusted walls and pillars, glittering mosaics, a marble inlaid floor covered with 375 marble-mosaic tombstone slabs, eye-catching paintings, colorful ceiling frescoes, numerous replicas of the four-armed, eight-pointed Maltese Cross, and oh, so much more.

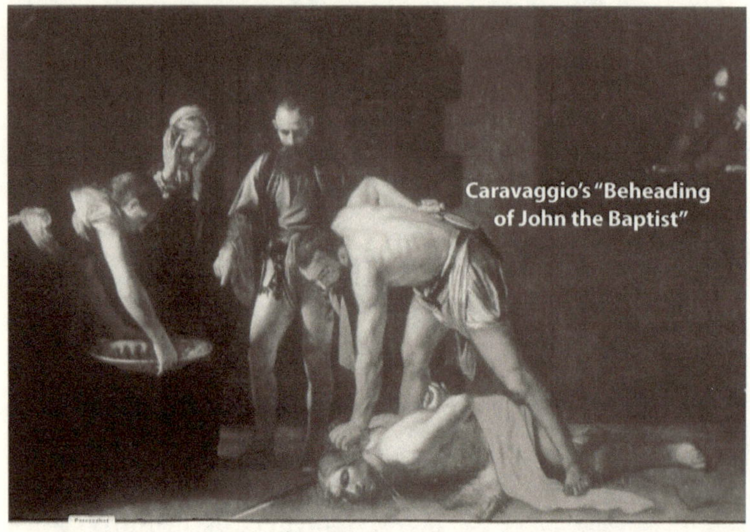

The cathedral has eight chapels allocated to the various *langues* (based on the noble knights' ethno-linguistic divisions) of the Knights of Malta and one dedicated to Our Lady of Philermos. Judging by the ostentatious décor, each langue was determined to out-do the others. Although the Knights had begun as a humble service organization in Jerusalem in the 11th century, by the time they remodeled this building they had clearly transformed themselves into something else. The Oratory has two impressive paintings by Caravaggio: the huge and thought-provoking painting "The Beheading of John the Baptist" and "St. Jerome Writing." There are other paintings as well.

You may find the Co-Cathedral an awe-inspiring, magnificent example of High Baroque, powerful in a dazzling kind of way. We found it a visual assault.

There is one room, however, that we found to be powerful in a different way. Located at the end of the corridor to the right side of the altar is the Chapel of Our Lady of Philermos/Chapel of the Blessed Sacrament. The entrance is often closed off, but if you are permitted to go in, you may be pleasantly surprised. The bustling, glitzy "look at me!" energy of the rest of the Co-Cathedral is instantly left behind, and you enter into a space that encourages peaceful contemplation.

A side note: Although the Knights of Malta were warriors, the Sacred Feminine was also important to them. The Virgin Mary was their patroness, and it's been said that St. Catherine of Alexandria was also their patroness. Note the altar painting of St. Catherine of Alexandria in the impressive baroque Chapel of the *Langue* of Italy. She is patroness of scholars and philosophers, among others. Because no mention is made of Catherine until the 9th century, many modern scholars think her life story was borrowed from the life of the Greek pagan Hypatia of Alexandria. Hypatia was a prominent Neoplatonic philosopher, mathematician, astronomer, and popular teacher who lived in 4th century Alexandria. She was brutally slaughtered by a mob of fanatical Christian monks. The legend of St. Catherine conveniently reverses the role of Christians and pagans. Perhaps the Knights' devotion to St. Catherine carried a hidden message about Hypatia and secret esoteric practices. Perhaps.

Our Experience in the Co-Cathedral

Elyn's Experience: Following advice we had been given by Freddy Silva, we sought out the Chapel of the Holy Sacrament/Our Lady of Philermos. It was blocked by a rope, but I asked politely if we could enter to pray, and we were allowed in. Ah.... What a wonderful, peaceful place. I knelt on the little kneeling chair in front of the altar and closed my eyes in meditation. Within moments, a fountain of energy flowed up through me and out the top of my head, clearing my "central channel." I have no idea where that energy came from. Maybe I was kneeling on an energy vortex. Maybe I was picking up energy from something else. Freddy thought there had been an ancient temple at this location and that its center was under the Chapel of the Holy Sacrament. Maybe so.

Entry Information

Entrance requires purchasing a ticket, which includes a personal audio guide and a visit to the Caravaggio paintings. Check open hours and prices at https://www.stjohnscocathedral.com/.

Getting There

St. John's Co-Cathedral is in the center of the old town of Valletta, central Malta, 5 miles from the international airport.

While you are in Valletta, don't miss visiting the National Museum of Archaeology. Most of the displays haven't been updated for decades, and some contain questionable reconstructions and hypotheses. Nonetheless, it is well worth taking a few hours to be in the presence of the original decorated blocks, altars, screens, and figurines that were removed from many of the megalithic temples and brought to the museum for safekeeping. The museum is included in the Heritage Malta Multisite Pass. http://heritagemalta.org/.

Catacombs in Malta — Going underground once again

Just like the ancient Maltese 6,000 years ago, more modern Maltese also buried their dead in rock-cut tombs. The numerous catacombs on Malta were subterranean burial places for Christians, pagans, and Jews, but mostly for Christians. We will describe four of the most important catacomb sites.

St. Paul's Catacombs, Rabat, central Malta

St. Paul's Catacombs are found in what has become the city of Rabat, located next to Mdina/Melita, the old Roman capitol of Malta. Roman law forbade burial within the city, so the catacombs were excavated nearby from the soft Globigerina Limestone. They are the oldest and most important Christian archaeological site on Malta. They are also the largest. Although they don't compare in size with the catacombs in Rome, they are quite impressive and eerie.

Carved out of soft sandstone, the underground maze of rooms, steps, and passageways covers 984 yards. They are named after the nearby Church of St. Paul, beneath which is St. Paul's Grotto. Tradition states that the saint spent time there after being shipwrecked on Malta.

St. Paul's Catacombs date from the last two centuries of the Roman period (around 330–535 CE) and were in use during much of the Byzantine period (535–870 CE). There are 22 other catacombs in the immediate vicinity. At one point the catacombs held some 1400 graves; 900 have survived. The graves vary in size and elaborahtion, and many were the graves of children.

At the center of the catacombs are two large halls, each with an *agape* (love) table hewn out of living rock. The tables are carved on pedestals, approximately 24" high and approximately 30" in diameter. *Agape* tables were important in late-Roman Christianity as the place to celebrate the communal "love feast." In Malta, the tables are a feature in numerous catacombs and were probably used for communal ritual meals after the burial of the deceased and/or for feasts commemorating dead relatives.

In the 13th century, an open space was recut in the catacombs and converted into a Christian shrine with murals. Later, the catacombs were used as a convenient place to store agricultural products. At some point, they fell into disrepair. Initial excavations, including clearing debris and a survey, were carried out in 1894.

Entry information

Tickets for St. Paul's Catacombs and the state-of-the-art interpretation center are available from http://heritagemalta. org and are included in the Heritage Malta Multisite Pass.

Getting there

Rabat is a suburb south of Mdina. Regular buses stop at Rabat bus station (0.12 mile, 200 yards south of Mdina Gate), and both "Hop On Hop Off" North Route bus services stop at Mdina Gate. It's approximately 11–13 minutes (0.6 mi) on foot from Mdina Gate to St. Paul's Catacombs. St. Agatha Catacombs are very close to St. Paul's Catacombs.

St. Agatha's Catacombs, Rabat, central Malta

St. Agatha's Catacombs were carved out of the soft local Globigerina limestone. They extend some 4900 sq. yards (or possibly 2600 sq. yards—the statistics vary) and include the tombs of 500 (or possibly 1000) people, the majority children. Many of the tombs are double, intended for the burial of two people (or at times more), sometimes side by side, sometimes separated by a thin stone partition. Most of them have stone pillows. The Catacombs include pagan, Jewish, and Christian graves in separate sections.

Its claim to fame is the artwork that decorates some of the subterranean stone walls of the catacombs and the nearby crypt. Roman Christian frescoes date from the 3rd–5th centuries; other frescoes date from the 12th century. The "Sancta Sanctorum," an underground, central shrine room located in the Catacombs, has a restored fresco dating from the 3rd century CE. The fresco includes a dove, a scallop shell, and an Alpha and Omega, among other motifs.

St. Agatha was a Sicilian martyr who, according to legend, lived in a small cave near the catacombs in 250 CE. She had fled her homeland to escape from marrying a high-ranking Roman official. The story goes that, after teaching Christianity for a short time on Malta, she decided to return to Sicily to bear witness to her faith. When she returned home, she was tortured and her breasts were cut off. She is often depicted holding her severed breasts on a plate.

St. Agatha's Historic Complex includes the crypt, catacombs, and museum. The crypt, supposedly where St. Agatha hid out, began as a natural cave. It was enlarged in the 4th and 5th centuries into an underground basilica. It contains an altar and numerous frescoes, some dating back to the 12th century and others to the 15th century. It was still in use for worship in the 17th century.

Entry information

Entry information is available at http://stagathamalta.com. Entry Fee. Entrance should be confirmed in advance by contacting catacombs@spmc.edu.mt or calling +356 2145 4503.

Getting there

Rabat is a suburb to the south of Mdina. Regular buses stop at Rabat bus station (0.12 mile, 200 yards south of Mdina Gate), and both "Hop On Hop Off" North Route buses stop at Mdina Gate. It's approximately 11–13 minutes (0.6 mile) on foot from Mdina Gate to St. Agatha's Catacombs. St. Agatha Catacombs are very close to St. Paul's Catacombs.

Ta' Bistra Catacombs, near Mosta, central Malta

Ta' Bistra Catacombs are located on the outskirts of Mosta, half way between the ancient town of Melita/Mdina and the once-important harbor of Salina. They were built sometime during the 4th century and are the largest set of Paleo-Christian tombs and catacombs accessible beyond the confines of the Rabat. The site is 300' long and consists of 57 tombs laid out in 16 chambers.

Over the millennia, the catacombs suffered much abuse, including looting and quarrying. At one time, a traditional Maltese farmhouse was built over them, which damaged some of the ancient chambers. In addition, they were occasionally "repurposed" as an animal pen. During WWII the catacombs were used as an air-raid shelter. Nonetheless, there remains much to see, including pilaster spiral decorations and a well-preserved *agape* table.

Heritage Malta has recently completed a visitor's center with a state-of-the-art canopy cover that enables people to explore the catacombs for the most part "above" ground.

Entry information

Entry is included with the Heritage Malta Multisite Pass. The Catacombs are not open every day, so it is important to check the schedule before going. See http://heritagemalta.org.

Getting there

Regular buses go to Mosta, as do both "Hop On Hop Off" North Route bus services. The Catacombs are a 20–24 minute walk (about 0.9 mile) from The Rotunda Square, Mosta.

While in Mosta, don't miss the powerful Mosta Rotunda (p. 171). The Wied il-Ghasel and St. Paul the Hermit's Chapel (see p. 165) are also close by. St. Paul the Hermit's Chapel is approx. 1.25–1.5 miles from Mosta Rotunda.

Salina Catacombs, Naxxar, northern Malta

These catacombs are located near the Church of the Annunciation, Salina, on the outskirts of Naxxar, in northern Malta near Qawra, to the east of St. Paul's Bay. In all, there are five hypogea, cut into the vertical face of a quarry and opening onto a low ridge facing a now-lost Roman harbor. The catacombs were in use between 500–1000 CE. Although smaller than St. Agatha's or St. Paul's Catacombs, they contain a number of canopied graves with elaborate relief decorations and an *agape* table. Some of the carvings resemble the double spiral oculi found at Tarxien and other ancient Maltese temples.

Entry information

Salina Catacombs are managed by Heritage Malta and are not currently open to visitors. We have included them as another example of the plethora of underground burial sites and the surprising continuity—or, more accurately, reappearance—of spiral motifs.

Controversies

These rock-cut tombs and underground passages are eerie, atmospheric, evocative—and somewhat reminiscent of Xagħra and Ħal Saflieni Hypogea. Both the Catacombs and Hypogea were subterranean burial places. Both were used for ceremonies by the living. The ancient Maltese temple builders constructed elaborate subterranean shrines and decorated the walls, and so did early and medieval Christians.

We are fascinated by the "discontinuous" practice of below-ground ceremony and ritual on Malta during 5,000 years (3500 BCE–1500 CE). We say "discontinuous" because the temple builders, who built the Hypogea, suddenly disappeared from Malta around 2500 BCE and were replaced by a completely different Bronze Age culture. Which, in turn, was replaced by other cultures, including the Phoenician,

Greek, and Roman. These people began to carve out the catacombs. Malta was depopulated in the 9th century, only to be repopulated in the 11th century by Christians from Sicily. They continued to use the underground shrines, if not for burial than at least for worship.

Many researchers assume that the Ħal Saflieni Hypogeum "Holy of Holies" and the associated 5,500-year-old burial practices are indicative of ancestor worship or, even, a religion based on a so-called cult of death. They have stated that the Hypogeum obviously demonstrates worship of the Great Mother in her chthonic, Underworld form.

Even though subterranean celebratory meals were being held in the Christian Catacombs in the presence of the dead, nobody would assert that Christianity was a death cult or that it involved ancestor worship. And, while there are many statues of the Virgin Mary beside the altars, nobody would declare that the religious practices were dedicated to the Great Mother in her Underworld manifestation.

This disparity in interpretation makes us reflect on what we think we know. It shows how important supporting evidence is. It demonstrates, once again, that we bring many (often unconscious) assumptions to our interpretation of prehistoric sites, ancient ritual practices, and belief systems.

St. Paul the Hermit Chapel, Wied il-Ghasel, Mosta Valley, central Malta — Bees, fresh water, and an ancient sacred site

Wied il-Ghasel means Valley (Wied) of Honey. It is 8.5 miles long and is part of one of Malta's most important water-catchment areas. During the rainy season, the valley is filled with pools and streams. Many species of flora, some endemic to Malta, thrive in this protected valley. There are also carob, fig, and olive trees. According to local folklore, bees built their hives in the cracks in the limestone cliffs and, in some places, the honey was so bountiful that it trickled out into the valley. Hence its name.

Three wayside chapels are found along this length of the Mosta Valley. One is dedicated to the Shipwreck of St. Paul, another to Ta' I-Isperanza (Our Lady of Hope), and the third to Saint Paul the Hermit, the "first" Christian hermit. [Note: Although Jerome considered Paul the first Christian hermit, today St. Anthony of Egypt is usually given that accolade.] We will focus on the powerful Chapel of Saint Paul the Hermit.

As one walks down the valley, the chapel becomes visible on the side of the cliff-face, sheltered inside a natural limestone cavern. Stone steps gradually lead up from the valley floor to the chapel. The cream-colored stone chapel was built in 1656 on the site of an older one of unknown date. The chapel was abandoned at some point, restored and slightly modified in the 1920s, then abandoned again, and, more recently, restored.

The story told about the origin of the chapel is the following. Centuries ago, a holy man named Korradu lived in the cave. One day, he chided some shepherds on their immoral lifestyle. They concocted a nefarious plan: they would have a young woman of loose morals wash her clothes in a nearby spring. She would pretend to call for help. If the hermit didn't help her, he would be accused of lack of charity; if he did help her, he would be charged with licentious behavior.

They put their plan into action, and the hermit ran to the girl's rescue. That was all the excuse the shepherds needed. They hurled insults and stones at him. He fled to the seashore, but they followed him. Then a miracle occurred. He spread his mantle on the water, stepped on it, and was carried over the waters to Gozo. He lived the rest of his life near the Church of the Virgin Mary at Qala, where he was later buried.

In penance (and repentance), the shepherds built a small church to St. Paul the Hermit in the cave where Korradu had lived. The current church replaced it in 1656.

The annual feast day of the saint (January 15) is celebrated at the wayside chapel, and numerous people participate. Another feast day, the Feast of our Lady of Grace, is also celebrated there.

The church is constructed with a rectangular nave. Currently, it has one main altar and a painting depicting St. Paul the Hermit and St. Anthony of Egypt. The painting is a copy of the one that was stolen in 1988 but later recovered. For safekeeping, the original is now kept in Mosta Rotunda Church.

There is an opening in the fourth bay in the north wall of the church that leads to a small, rock-cut chapel to the Virgin Mary and a small vestry beyond. Inside this chapel is a marble altar with a painting depicting the Virgin Mary and a stone basin that holds water that naturally drips from the overhanging limestone rocks.

There are two such stone basins at St. Paul the Hermit's church. One is inside the chapel of the Virgin; the other is outside, to the west of the entrance to the church. A dark varnish-like stain spreads across part of the overhanging rock, caused by millennia of minerals dissolving through the limestone. We presume that this is the water that St. Paul the Hermit drank. In the past, the water was considered to have medicinal properties.

It is likely that this church, like many other churches, has been superimposed on a much more ancient sacred site associated with a female deity (see p. 180). Evidence includes the medicinal water dripping from the overhanging rocks and the rock-cut chapel currently dedicated to the Virgin. Another Maltese example of this connection between water and a female deity is the Grotto of Our Lady in Mellieħa, where a statue of Mary stands inside a limestone cave, surrounded by a pool of water fed by an underground spring (see p. 177).

Our Experience in the Chapel

Elyn's Experience: We carefully descended the steps cut into the steep hillside and began walking into the Valley of Honey. The gentle mist turned into a downpour. Soon we heard a buzzing sound, even through the rain. Our government-mandated Maltese guide asserted that we were hearing the buzzing of bees, from which the valley got its name, even though it was raining. Gary was convinced that we were hearing the resonant frequency of the valley, just as we had heard the resonance frequency in the Oracle Room of the Hypogeum. Whatever the source, it added to the evocative atmosphere.

The valley was a mix of stark eroding limestone and lush spring flowers. Wet and bedraggled, we sloshed through the rain. We were relieved to reach the chapel and find shelter from the down-

pour under the cavernous overhang. I leaned back against the stones and gradually was lulled into a meditative state. The bees buzzing (if that's what we heard) reminded me that, in Classical Greece, the priestesses of Demeter, goddess of agriculture, mother of Persephone, were called Melissas—Greek for "honey bees." And I remembered the beehive-like ochre designs painted on the ceiling in Ħal Saflieni Hypogeum. Bees... humming... Earth goddesses... water dripping from the stones in the cavern, like honey dripping from the hillsides... I felt certain that this had been a sacred site long before Christianity came to the islands.

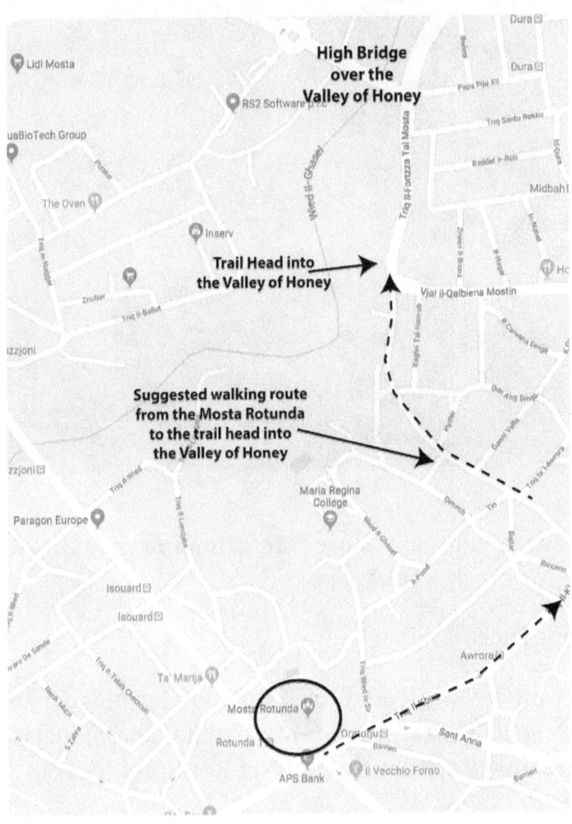

Entry Information

It is not advisable to walk in the valley during pouring rain. After the deluge, the stairsteps we had walked down into the valley were covered with a torrent of water running off the plateau. We had to find another way to get back up the hill.

The church is usually closed. Information may be available on http://thechurchinmalta.org.

Getting There

The Wied il-Ghasel and St. Paul the Hermit's Chapel are very close to Mosta, north-central Malta. The chapel is about 1.25–1.5 miles on foot from Mosta Rotunda.

There are several routes to St. Paul the Hermit's Chapel, which you can find by going to Google maps, but Google won't lead you through the valley. We suggest the following walking route from the Mosta Rotunda to the Valley of Honey. This route will give you the most dramatic view of the Valley and the Chapel of St. Paul the Hermit, but it should be attempted only in good weather and with good hiking shoes. (Thank you, Martina Brtnicka, Photo Blogger, http://www.maltatina.com, for sending us photos of the trailhead.)

Find the trailhead by following the map and photo provided here. Descend the trail, which is a rough trail with occasional steps. When you get into the valley you will see the high bridge on your right. Take the trail that leads under the high bridge. Once you have walked further into the valley, you will see the chapel ahead, nestled under an overhang, about half-way up the cliff. Follow the steps that lead up to the chapel. Return by the same route.

Use good judgment. The valley can become quite wet during and following a rainstorm. The trail is uneven and rocky, so take care—and follow these directions at your own risk.

Mosta Dome (AKA Mosta Rotunda), Mosta, central Malta — A geometrical marvel

The gigantic dome of Mosta's parish church, dedicated to the Assumption of the Virgin, is visible from most locations on Malta. Mosta Rotunda is famous for many things other than its size, including its miraculous escape from destruction in WWII. A German bomb pierced the dome in 1942 while 300 parishioners were waiting to hear Mass (or maybe they were seeking shelter from the air raid. Or maybe both). Miraculously, the bomb skidded across the floor but didn't detonate. Equally miraculous, the bomb didn't destroy the dome. A replica bomb can be seen to the left of the altar in the sacristy.

Another, earlier miracle is that no one was injured during the erection of the dome. The entire construction was done without any scaffolding, either to enable the parishioners to continue worshipping in the existing church or to save constructions costs. Or both. At any rate, the builders put their faith in God, and they were not disappointed. The church was built with money raised by local people and with voluntary labor.

The Dome was designed by the Maltese architect Giorgio Grognet de Vassé. It was built between 1833–60, erected over a smaller, existing church, which may have been built over an ancient temple site. Grognet de Vassé chose to design a round, neo-Classical church inspired by the Roman Pantheon rather than one based on a Latin cross. His plan was highly controversial because he used the floorplan of a pagan temple for a Christian church.

The gigantic dome has an outer diameter of 177' and soars to a height of over 197'. The interior diameter of 122' makes it the fourth-largest unsupported dome in Europe. The other three are Rome's Pantheon, Rome's St. Peter's, and Gozo's Xewkija Basilica, which replaced Mosta's in third place in 1971. Gozo's dome is 246' high. The people of Mosta, however, are insistent that their dome beats that of Gozo if you measure the width rather than the height.

One of the reasons that Mosta Dome is a powerful place is its splendid cupola. The oculus (the skylight opening) at the top of the cupola is surrounded by 32 white petals painted on top of and overlapping 32 golden petals painted on top of a blue background. Radiating out from the white and gold rings surrounding the petals are numerous square, gold-framed, blue lozenges, each with a gold, 5-petaled flower inside. The 5-petaled flower stands for the Virgin Mary, but the number 5 is also associated with the star (and goddess) Venus.[132]

Each lozenge is precisely placed on the white background of the dome. Visually, it appears that the lozenges are arranged in rays, each composed of 16 lozenges, that curve gracefully out from the center opening. The lozenge rays alternate with rays made up of 16 small, gold, 5-petaled flowers. Altogether, they form a mesmerizing pattern of overlapping and intersecting curves.

Francis Aloisio has pointed out that the petal pattern is based on 4, 8, 16, 32—the same pattern that can be seen in the 32-petal design in the floor.[133] The side entrances, one dedicated to St. Joseph and one to the Mater Dolorosa, both have flower patterns in the center of the floor but based on a different number.

He writes that "This site has the greatest vibrational energy on the island as the church stands on the matrix of all prehistoric temples."[134] The master dowser Hamish Miller dowsed 32 "energy" petals radiating out from Mosta Dome.[135] We don't know whether Hamish's energy petals were influenced by the cupola design or the design was intuitively influenced by the energy lines.

According to Aloisio, all three domed churches on Malta (Xewkija on Gozo, and Mġarr and Mosta on Malta) are built over ancient temple sites.[136] That wouldn't be unusual since it was standard Christian practice from the 6th century CE to repurpose pagan sacred sites—just as it had been standard pagan practice before.

One thing is certain, however. Whoever planned this interior decoration was a serious practitioner of sacred geometry. To our eyes, the cupola decoration resembles the pecked patterns on the orthostats in Mnajdra Temple South. Granted, the Mnajdra designs are much less intricate and their arrangement much less refined—but, after all, they were made nearly 5,500 years earlier by people using stone and antler tools to peck patterns into limestone.

Our Experience in Mosta Dome

Elyn's Experience: We walked into the church via the Dolorosa side entry. I immediately felt as if someone had knocked me over. The energy inside was that strong, that palpable. My head felt like the top was blown open. Our guide indicated that he likes to come to this place and stand on the central petal flower to recharge. Hmmm. What recharges him seemed to "discharge" me.

That's how it is in powerful places. Each person will have a different experience of the energies. The difference is a complex interaction between (1) the powerful place itself, which differs in energy depending on the time of day, the moon cycle, and the seasons, among other factors (including what ritual or gathering has just taken place at the powerful place), and (2) the person experiencing the energies, who also differs in energy depending on the time of day, the moon cycle, the seasons, their health, their mood, etc. In addition, some people energetically "prefer" one kind of energy to another. Perhaps their personal frequency is a better match with the specific location. I get easily thrown off-balance by standing on an energy vortex, but other people thrive on them.

Entry Information

Mosta Rotunda is an active church. Proper attire is required. There is a charge of 2€/pp for tourists who want to visit the church, the sacristy, and the bomb museum. Check the website for opening hours. https://mostachurch.com/lang/en/informazzjoni-ghat-turisti/.

Getting There

Numerous regular buses pass through Mosta, as do both "Hop On Hop Off" North Route bus services. Mosta is 7 miles from Valletta and 2.7 miles from Mdina. The Valley of Honey and St. Paul the Hermit Chapel is about a ½ hour walk from Mosta Dome (see p. 165). Ta' Bistra Catacombs are on the outskirts.

The Sanctuary of Our Lady of Mellieħa and The Grotto of the Madonna, Mellieħa, northwest Malta — An ancient goddess shrine or two?

Mellieħa (mell-ee-ha) is a picturesque town on a ridge located between St. Paul's Bay and Mellieħa Bay. Mellieħa Bay is the longest sandy beach on Malta, famous for its soft white sand and warm shallow waters. Temple Period sites were recorded southwest of the town, but they disappeared long ago. What makes Mellieħa powerful today are two shrines dedicated to Our Lady.

The 19th century Parish Church of the Nativity of Our Lady perches on a prominent rocky spur overlooking the bay, on the northern edge of town. Attached to it, at a slightly lower level, is the much older Sanctuary of Our Lady of Mellieħa. It is believed that St. Paul visited the grotto when he was shipwrecked on Malta in 60 CE. A fresco of the Madonna and Child, painted on the rock wall of the sanctuary, is said to have been painted by St. Luke, who was shipwrecked along with St. Paul.

The Sanctuary of Our Lady of Mellieħa has been very important for centuries to Maltese sailors, and a pilgrims' way and pilgrims' hostels were associated with the site. It is entered via a large sheltering courtyard that seems to protect the space. The sanctuary was constructed by enlarging a natural grotto. Its stone walls are decorated with a profusion of ex-votos (votive offerings), including children's clothes and numerous framed paintings attesting to miraculous rescues from shipwreck. The sanctuary is said to be one of the oldest Christian shrines in the world. Clearly this is a powerful place.

Votive offerings in the Sanctuary of Our Lady of Mellieħa

Very near this sacred site is an even more powerful place, one that is undoubtedly even older: The Grotto of the Madonna—or, as it is called in Maltese, Il-Madonna Tal-Ghar, located deep within a natural limestone cave. To reach it, the visitor crosses the street, goes through an imposing entryway in a stone wall, walks down a long flight of wide steps, passes through an entrance in a limestone façade, walks down another flight of steps in a rough-hewn tunnel, and then, at last, enters the Grotto of the Madonna. The journey takes you from daylight and the surface world into darkness and the Underworld. You can imagine that it also takes you from the superficial into your own inner depths.

At the back of the cavern is a spring that is reputed to have healing powers. Surrounded by a candle-laden metal screen, a statue of Our Lady and Child stands on a rough stone pillar in the midst of a pool of this special water. Baby clothes, letters, rosaries, photos, and other votive offerings express gratitude for conception, perhaps for healing, and include requests for people who have died. When we were first there, one wall was covered with ex-votos, but the last time we were there, the offerings had been culled and organized. Only a few letters and baby clothes, neatly covered in plastic bags and attached to a display board, attested to the Virgin's miracles and the devotees' faith.

Millennia ago, fresh water was a valued and rare commodity on often-arid Malta. We can imagine that this reliable source of fresh water deep within this cave was treated with great respect. Perhaps it did, indeed, have curative powers.

Feminine deities are often associated with water and with the Earth. Perhaps this cave was sacred and dedicated to the bountiful Goddess, giver of life in the form of water and represented by the Earth, whose "body" we are entering in this subterranean grotto. This is the same Goddess who, in later centuries, morphed into "Our Lady," the Virgin Mary, whose statue stands in the center of the spring.[137] St. Paul the Hermit Chapel, p. 165, is another example. We describe another example in our guidebook *Powerful Places in Brittany*. A holy well issues from under the altar at the Basilica of Our Lady, Le Folgoët. The fountain is outside, and pilgrims still come to take the miraculous water.

Our Experience at the Grotto

Gary's Experience: The grotto was deep under the hillside. Even though a skylight opened into the grotto, candles added a mysterious quality to the light. Our guide said it was a very special place for him—he came here to soak up the light and recharge.

Elyn's Experience: We entered deep into the body of the Earth, into a womb-like cave lit by flickering candles and a filtered ray of sunshine. Our Lady stood on a pillar, surrounded by life-giving waters. The generosity of the Earth, the Earth Mother, providing fresh drinkable water in this arid land, was palpable. I could hear the sound of bubbling water and almost taste its refreshing goodness. While we sat in stillness, soaking up the atmosphere of this powerful holy place, a man came into the grotto and, with difficulty, managed to fill a plastic bottle with the waters welling up in the spring.

Entry Information

These are active churches and pilgrimage sites. Check the website for details and schedules http://www.Mellieha.com/parish_church.htm. It appears that The Grotto of The Madonna is open 24 hours/day.

Getting There

Mellieħa is in northwest Malta, between Mellieħa and St. Paul's Bays. Regular buses run from Valletta.

Travel Tips

Most people speak English, often with a Maltese accent. Malta is very hot and an extremely popular tourist destination in summer (late June–mid September), so planning your trip for off-season is a wise idea.

Airlines: Malta International Airport is in Luqa, 5 miles southeast of Valletta, the capital, on the island of Malta. Numerous buses and taxis can take you from the airport to your destination.

Buses: There are three bus services: open-topped "Hop On Hop Off" buses run by http://MaltaSightseeing.com and http://CitySightseeingMalta.com, both of which provide audio commentary, and an inexpensive island-wide "regular" bus service (http://maltabybus.com).

We have included information about bus services for reaching the sites described in the book. However, please double-check transportation schedules because they are subject to change. Also note that, regardless of schedule, the bus may not show up at the scheduled time because it has been caught in a traffic jam, or got behind schedule, or....

You can reach numerous places on the island via bus but not places that are out of the way. A taxi is often useful, and many Maltese use the ecab phone app (http://ecabs.com.mt). Because of differences in pronunciation, we have often found it useful to ask a museum clerk or restaurant host to call a taxi for us.

Driving: Malta was a British colony, so driving is on the left-hand side. Drivers prefer to drive in the shade—wherever they find it—and often pull out in front of you unexpectedly. In addition, there are numerous unanticipated diversions and detours, and road signage can be confusing or non-existent.

It is much less stressful (in general) to have an experienced Maltese driver as your conductor than to risk navigating the traffic on your own.

Once our taxi driver became so frustrated by urban traffic that he left the main thoroughfare and drove down twisting one-way streets and alleys. He finally arrived at what appeared to be an off-ramp from the highway, which he proceeded to use as an on-ramp while reassuring us that "everything is OK! Don't worry."

Traffic, especially on Malta near Valletta, is often heavy and there are traffic jams. Allow plenty of extra time if you are trying to get to the airport for a flight or have reservations to visit a site for a particular time. Depending on the time of day, a 15-minute-long trip can take up to an hour.

Ferries: Travel between Malta and Gozo is easily accomplished via an inexpensive, 25-minute-long Gozo Channel Company ferry ride (http://gozochannel.com). Ferries travel frequently between Cirkewwa (Malta) and Mġarr Harbor

(Gozo). Buses and taxis connect with the sailing schedule. Or, if you prefer to have even less hassle, for an additional fee you can schedule a taxi to take you from Malta, onto the ferry, and then to your destination on Gozo—and vice versa.

Entry Tickets: Several locations/events (e.g., spring equinox sunrise at Mnajdra Temple, access to Ħal Saflieni Hypogeum) require advance ticket purchases. This is best done online, far in advance of your visit. You can also purchase a Multisite Pass from Heritage Malta (http://heritagemalta.org) that will save you money if you are planning to visit a number of Heritage Malta sites. Remember: always allow plenty of extra time to get to your destination if you have an advanced reservation.

Afterword

Malta attracts conflict and controversy like a magnet. Theories swirl around its prehistory and ancient temples. The lack of continuity of habitation through the millennia probably contributes to this, as does destruction from warfare and colonization. There is no ongoing mythic memory that can be explored for deeper insights. There is much that is unknown, and much that is unknowable, but that doesn't mean we don't want some reliable answers. We have discovered during our research that what constitutes "reliable" for one person is pure speculation to another, and what constitutes consensus for one group is open to debate to another.

We began this book with a series of questions. Who built these enormous, complex megalithic temples? How did they build them? Why did they build them? What purpose did they serve? Where did they gain the knowledge to create the astronomical alignments at Mnajdra and Ħaġar Qim (among other temples)? There is nothing like these temples anywhere else—not at that time (before Stonehenge, before the Great Pyramid) and not elsewhere.

The archaeological consensus that Sicilian farmers came to Malta and suddenly started building colossal constructions seems inadequate and incomplete to us. Do the alternative theories explain the situation better? We have our doubts. Nobody has come up with satisfying answers. We need more data.

Did people settle on Malta much earlier than the archaeological consensus? Probably, but there doesn't appear to be any reliable evidence available at this time. The slim evidence that might exist for earlier habitation appears to have been contaminated, misplaced, or is considered unworthy of further exploration. This includes possible Paleolithic artifacts, rock art, teeth, and (even) long-headed skulls. We can imagine the Heritage Malta personnel saying to themselves—"Oh no—not those questions again!" We would like researchers to re-evaluate the available data instead of dismissing it and the querents out of hand.

Was the Ħal Saflieni Hypogeum only a cemetery filled with a jumble of earth and bones? Of course not. It was a multi-purpose underground ritual space used for many purposes, bringing the living and dead into power-full proximity. Was it only used for mortuary rituals? We don't think so, given that it was designed to mimic above-ground temples, given that the winter solstice sun shone into the Holy of Holies, given the pecked and painted decorations on the walls and ceilings, and given the "Sleeping Lady" lying on her side, dreaming. We think it was used for initiation and dream-incubation rituals, along with ceremonies for the dead. But we can't prove that.

Was there a Goddess-worshipping culture on Malta? Probably. But again, we don't know. Are the "Fat Lady" statuettes and the temples proof of this? To begin with, we do not think they are all Fat Ladies. We think they are obese statuettes of usually indeterminate gender, often with removable heads. This gender fluidity raises fascinating questions about the ancient Maltese concept of the Divine and how they expressed it in their temples and daily lives. Do the multi-lobed temples represent the body of the Goddess? We think they were designed to express something about the nature of Divinity, but we don't know what.

What about the cart-ruts? To quote Winston Churchill (1939), they are "a riddle wrapped in a mystery, inside an enigma." Exploring them is an excellent way to enjoy a day out on Malta, but nobody has successfully explained them.

Malta is like a Rorschach test. The way you interpret a temple, a statue, or a cart-rut says as much about you as about what you are seeing. Fact-based archaeology? Intuitive channeling? Much-needed historical re-evaluation? Evidence of a long-lost Atlantian civilization? Together, these theories create a rich mélange of possibilities.

We have an approach-avoidance relationship with Malta. Every time we go there, we say we're never going back—the energy is unsettling, the controversies disconcerting, the landscape harsh. But we return, drawn back again and again to powerful places that are full of mystery and transformative energy. Despite our ambivalence, we have had profound, life-changing experiences on Malta that continue to reverberate in our daily lives.

Appendix 1: Maltese Pronunciation

The purpose of this brief guide is not to make you fluent in Malti (Maltese)—it is simply to provide a guide to how to pronounce the powerful places you may want to visit.

Maltese is written using Latin letters (rather than hieroglyphs, Cyrillic, or Arabic script, for example). However, there are some tricks to know to pronounce the words correctly.

The Maltese alphabet contains 30 letters. 24 are consonants, 6 are vowels, and some are specific to Maltese. In addition, some letters are not pronounced the way an English speaker would expect. Some are more guttural, and some are usually "silent" but lengthen the vowel sounds around them.

The letters that are different in pronunciation are:

Ċ: pronounced like "ch" in "chat"

Ġ: pronounced like "j" in "jar" or "g" in "gem"

Għ: a silent single letter that prolongs the sound of a vowel before or after it (loghba = lowwba)

H: silent vowel, prolongs sound of whatever vowel follows it; if at end of word, pronounced like h with bar

Ħ: "Kh" as in Khan -- a guttural throat-clearing sound ending in "h"

Ie: a diphthong, pronounced like "eee-eh" in "yield"

J: pronounced as "y" in "yes"

Q: either silent or a kind of glottal stop, or as in "queue"

X: pronounced like "sh" in "shiny" or "shade"

Z: pronounced as "z" in "pizza" or "ts" "cats"

Ż: pronounced like "z" in "zoo"

(Credit is given to http://learn101.org/maltese_alphabet.
php and https://www.omniglot.com/writing/maltese.htm
and http://mylanguages.org/maltese_alphabet.php for this
information.)

Here are some of the powerful places on Malta with the correct pronunciation.

Birżebbuġa – beer-zeb-boo-ja, "Well of the Olives." Għar
Dalam Cave and Museum is nearby.

Cirkewwa – cheer-keh-wah

Dwejra – dway-rah

Ġgantija Temples – dje-gant-ee-ya (also pronounced as ja-
gun-tee-yah), "Giantess"

Għar Dalam Cave and Museum – aar-da-lam, "Cave of Darkness"

Ħaġar Qim – adge-ar eem, (though may also be pronounced
adge-ar keem), "Standing Stones"

Ħal – hull (Ħal Saflieni....)—Hal means "village," from Maltese "Rahal."

In-Naxxar — In-nahsh-shar

Ix-Xlendi— ish-shlen-dee

Marsaxloxx – marsa-shlock, "southeasterly harbor"

Mġarr – mm-jarr

Mnajdra – mm-nigh-dra

Tarxien – tar-sheen

Xagħra – shaa-ra, one of Gozo's largest villages. Ġgantija Temples and Xagħra Stone Circle are located there.

Appendix 2: Archaeological Phases

This is a Powerful Places Guidebook, not an archaeological guide. However, a little background information (however provisional) will help make sense of the chronology of sacred sites on Malta.

Maltese prehistory is divided into 11 overlapping phases that are named after sites where datable or sequential material was found. The phases are not limited to the sites where they were first found. For example, the East Temple at Skorba "belongs" to the Tarxien Phase, although it is not at Tarxien, and the West Temple at Skorba "belongs" to the Saflieni Phase, although it is not at Saflieni. In addition, recent research by Prof. Caroline Malone and her group at Belfast is changing some of these dates.

The following is a simplified description of these phases. (See David H. Trump and Anthony Bonanno for slightly different dates.)

Neolithic (5000–4200 BCE)
Għar Dalam (5000–4500 BCE)
Grey Skorba (4500–4400 BCE)
Red Skorba (4400–4100 BCE)

Temple Period (4100–2500 BCE)
Zebbug (4100–3800 BCE)
Mġarr (3850–3550 BCE)
Ġgantija (3600–3150 BCE)
Saflieni (3300–3000 BCE)
Tarxien (3150–2500 BCE)

Malta appears to have been briefly uninhabited from 2500–2350 BCE, or maybe from 2350–2000 BCE, if Prof. Malone's dates are correct.

Bronze and Iron Age Period
Tarxien Cemetery (2350–1475 BCE)
Borg In-Nadur (1500–700 BCE)
Bahrija (900–700 BCE)

Punic/Roman
Phoenician 700–550 BCE)
Punic (550–218 BCE)
Roman Republic (218–27 BCE)
Roman Empire (27 BCE–535 CE)
Byzantine (535–870 CE)

Arab
(870–1091 CE)

Appendix 3: Glossary

Apse: A semi-circular or D-shaped chamber, often found on either side of a central corridor.

Baldachin or baldaquin: A ceremonial canopy of stone, metal, or fabric over an altar, throne, or doorway.

Basilica: A Greek word that refers to "royal house." It also refers to a church that has been given special ecclesiastical privileges by the pope.

BCE: Before Current Era; a neutral replacement for BC (Before Christ).

Bronze Age: Prehistoric period in which copper and bronze (a copper alloy) were used instead of stone for tools and for weapons. Follows the Neolithic and is followed by the Iron Age.

C-14, Carbon Dating, or Carbon-14 Dating: Radiocarbon dating is a method for determining the age of an object. It can only be used on an object that contains organic material. It is based on the properties of radiocarbon, a radioactive isotope of carbon, which decays over time. The method was developed in the late 1940s.

CE: Current Era; a neutral replacement for AD (Anno Domini).

Collective burial: Burial practice in which successive burials join earlier ones. Earlier bones are pushed to the back of the burial chamber or removed to make room for subsequent burials. May include "secondary burial," in which the body is initially buried in one place and then, after the flesh has decayed, the bones are gathered together and buried in a communal/collective burial site. Examples are Ħal Saflieni and Xagħra Hypogeum.

Corbelling: A roof made out of stone slabs, each course or row set a bit further in toward the center, progressively overlapping to create a vault or dome. Extant examples of megalithic corbelling are found in Newgrange, Ireland, and Maes Howe, Scotland.

Cremation: Burning the dead and burying only the ashes.

Dolmen: Prehistoric megalithic structure made of upright stones topped with a large, horizontal capstone. Usually, originally covered by earth, perhaps stones, but over the millennia the covering has worn away. Found throughout Europe. Most date to 4000–3000 BCE; the ones on Malta are somewhat more recent—2500–1500 BCE.

Ex-voto: An offering to a saint or to a divinity, given in fulfilment of a vow. A votive offering. Can include texts describing the miracle, or copies (in wax, metal, etc.) of the relevant body part, or directly related items such as crutches.

Heliacal: The rising of a celestial object at the same time as the sun, or its first visible rising after a period of invisibility due to conjunction with the sun.

Hypogeum (pl. Hypogea): An underground temple; a subterranean tomb.

Iconography, iconographic: The visual images and symbols used in a work of art, specific to that culture and its artistic tradition.

Libation hole: Vertical hole pierced into paving slab, as at a threshold—or sometimes found on other flat stone blocks. Assumed to have been used to receive liquid offerings (libations), so they could "reach" the deities or ancestors.

Marian Shrine: A shrine or chapel dedicated to the Virgin Mary.

Megalith: Literally, a very "large stone" used in building. If free-standing, often called a menhir.

Menhir: A large, free-standing, upright stone.

Mystery School: Specializes in teaching a variety of occult subjects including metaphysics, alchemy, personal transformation, spiritual initiation, etc. Usually requires secrecy from initiates, so little is known about the content.

Neanderthal: An extinct species or subspecies of archaic humans in the genus Homo, who lived within Eurasia from circa 400,000 until 40,000 years ago and interbred with Anatomically Modern Humans/Homo Sapiens.

Neolithic: Prehistoric time period when people primarily raised crops, had domesticated livestock, and used ground and flaked stone tools.

Ochre: A naturally occurring iron oxide. Ground and mixed with water, it was used as a reddish pigment on walls, sculptures, and bones. Usually associated with the sacred, with blood, and with death (and perhaps rebirth or the afterlife). It had to be imported to Malta.

Orthostat: Large, upright slab of stone used in building a wall. Not free-standing.

Paleolithic: Prehistoric time period when people relied on hunting and gathering for subsistence and only used flaked stone or bone for tools. It remains controversial whether Paleolithic humans lived on Malta.

Parvis: An enclosed area in front of a cathedral or church, typically surrounded with colonnades or porticoes.

Phoenician: People coming from what is now Lebanon. Normally refers to the timespan of 800–500 BCE.

Pitted decoration: Made by drilling shallow holes into the surface of a limestone block. The pockmarked, pecked holes vary in density and organization.

Pleistocene: Period that began about 2.6 million years ago and lasted until about 11,700 years ago. The most recent Ice Age occurred then, during which glaciers covered huge parts of the planet.

Porthole slab: A slab-like stone with a large central opening, which forms an entrance.

Precession of stars: Precession refers to the slow shift over time of the rising point in the east and setting point in the west of the fixed stars along the horizon.

Spiral: A curve emanating from a central point and getting larger as it revolves outward. It can curve either clockwise or counter-clockwise. It is both a natural phenomenon, found in snail shells, spiral galaxies, and tornados, and a mathematically derivable form. The spiral in various shapes and patterns (single, double, triple, interconnected, simple, "barbed," "fishtailed," etc.) is found throughout the world in ancient rock art.

Telluric energy line: An underground energy line that can be dowsed by experienced dowsers. There are different kinds of telluric energies, including "fire" lines and "water" lines, corresponding to naturally occurring underground features.

Temple Builder Period: approximately 4100–2500 BCE. It is divided into overlapping phases: Zebbug (4100–3800 BCE), Mġarr (3850–3550 BCE), Ġgantija (3600–3150 BCE), Ġgantija (3600–3150 BCE), Saflieni (3300–3000 BCE), and Tarxien (3200–2500 BCE).

Trilithon: A structure composed of two large upright stones supported by a horizontal lintel above. It may be a doorway or entrance, or it may be a structure that leads into another space or, as at Stonehenge, a series of trilithons form a circular structure.

Torba: A prehistoric Maltese floor surface resembling concrete. It was produced by crushing Globigerina limestone, spreading it over a rubble foundation, wetting it down, pounding it, wetting it, pounding it again, until a hard smooth surface was formed.

Tumulus: An earthen mound raised over a grave or graves—or over a dolmen, which might or might not have been a grave. Also known as a barrow, a burial mound, or a kurgan. Found throughout the world.

Notes

1   see http://powerfulplaces.com.

2   see Elizabeth Brown, *Dowsing – The Ultimate Guide for the 21ˢᵗ Century*. One of the best ways to develop sensitivity is through personal contact with a geomancer, dowser, or earth-energy aficionado. We have studied with Ferran Blasco (http://rochesteracupuncture.us), Sig Lonegren (http://www.avalon.co.nl/about/?lang=en), and Dominique Susani (https://bouldermasterbuilders.com).

3   Anthony Pace, *The Tarxien Temples—Tarxien*, Malta: Heritage Books, 2010, p. 8.

4   Nadia Fabri, *Għar Dalam—The Cave, The Museum, and the Garden,* Malta: Heritage Books, 2007.

5   Charles Savona-Ventura and Anton Mifsud, *Hasan's Cave,* Malta: Heritage Books, 2000, pp. 27–35.

6   David H. Trump, *Malta Prehistory and Temples*, 3d edition, Malta: Midsea Books Ltd., 2008, p. 25.

7   Caroline Malone research in newspaper article, 2018, https://www.timesofmalta.com/articles/view/20180316/life-features/700-years-added-to-maltas-history.673498

8   Anthony Bonanno, *The Archaeology of Malta & Gozo—5000 BC–AD 1091*, Malta: Heritage Malta, 2017, p. 5.

9   David H. Trump, *Malta Prehistory*, p. 25.

10   Arthur Keith, "Discovery of Neanderthal Man in Malta," 1918, *Nature*, 101, 404-405.

11   See Anton Mifsud article on Graham Hancock's website, https://grahamhancock.com/mifsuda2/; for a

longer account, see Anton and Simon Mifsud, *Dossier Malta*, 1997.

12   Anton Mifsud interview, 2016, https://www.time-sofmalta.com/articles/view/20160619/local/could-the-first-maltese-have-been-neanderthals.615901

13   Anton and Simon Mifsud, *Dossier Malta—Evidence for the Magdalenian*, Malta: Proprint Company Ltd., 1997.

14   Graham Hancock, *Underworld—The Mysterious Origins of Civilization*, New York: Three Rivers Press, 2003.

15   Francis X. Aloisio, private communication, 9 June 2019.

16   Lenie Reedijk, *Sirius—The Star of the Maltese Temples*, The Netherlands: Malet Books, 2018.

17   Lenie Reedijk, *Sirius*, pp. 14–15.

18   T. Eric Peet, *Rough Stone Monuments and Their Builders*, London and New York: Harper & Brothers, 1912, p. 156.

19   John Evans, quoted in Tore Lomsdalen, *Sky and Purpose in Prehistoric Malta: Sun, Moon, and Stars at the Temples of Mnajdra*, Ceredigion, Wales: Sophia Centre Press, University of Wales, 2014, p. xix.

20   Klaus Albrecht, *Malta's Temples—Alignments and Religious Motives*, 2nd edition in English, Potsam: Sven Nather Verlag, 2007.

21   Lenie Reedijk, *Sirius*, p. 105.

22   David H. Trump, *Malta Prehistory*, p. 156.

23   David H. Trump, *Malta Prehistory*, p. 43.

24   Klaus Albrecht, *Malta's Temples*.

25   Lenie Reedijk, *Sirius*.

26   See Anthony Bonanno, *The Archaeology of Malta & Gozo*, p. 18, and David H. Trump, *Malta Prehistory*, pp. 154–155.

27   Lenie Reedijk, *Sirius*.

28   Klaus Albrecht, *Malta's Temples*.

29   Klaus Albrecht, *Malta's Temples*.

30   Leni Reedijk, *Sirius*.

31   David H. Trump, *Malta: An Archaeological Guide*, London: Faber & Faber Ltd., 1972, pp. 157–158.

32   David H. Trump, *Malta Prehistory*, p. 102.

33   T. Eric Peet, *Rough Stone Monuments and Their Builders*, p. 173.

34   See Anthony Pace, *The Ħal Saflieni Hypogeum—Paola*, Malta: Heritage Books, 2004, pp. 27–29, for a detailed description of the illumination.

35   Anthony Pace, *The Ħal Saflieni Hypogeum*, p. 25.

36   Anton Mifsud et al., *Malta—Echoes of Plato's Island*, 2nd revised edition, Malta: The Prehistoric Society of Malta, 2001, p. 38.

37   T. Eric Peet, *Rough Stone Monuments and Their Builders*, p. 176.

38   David H. Trump, *Malta Prehistory*, pp. 130–131.

39   David H. Trump, *Malta: An Archaeological Guide*, p. 63.

40   Lenie Reedijk, *Sirius*, p. 31.

41   Anton and Simon Mifsud, *Dossier Malta*, pp. 168–173.

42   T. Eric Peet, *Rough Stone Monuments and Their Builders*, p. 175.

43   Freddy Silva, *The Missing Lands—Uncovering Earth's Pre-Flood Civilization*, 2019, p. 182.

44   Anton Mifsud and Charles Savona-Ventura, editors, *Facets of Maltese Prehistory*. Malta: Prehistoric Society of Malta, 1999.

45   Melanie Drury, 21 January 2019, "Elongated Heads" article, https://www.guidememalta.com/en/why-are-these-elongated-skulls-at-hal-saflieni-hypogeum-shrouded-in-mystery.

46   Lois Jessop, reprinted in https://borderlandsciences.org/journal/vol/17/n02/Jessop_Malta_Cavern_World.html.

47   Anthony Pace, *The Ħal Saflieni Hypogeum*, p. 40.

48   David H. Trump, *Malta Prehistory*, pp. 130–131.

49   Anthony Pace, *The Tarxien Temples*, p. 11.

50   David H. Trump, *Malta Prehistory*, p. 120.

51   quoted in Cheryl Straffon, "The Goddess in the Temple," Part 1, ND.

52   Anthony Pace, *The Tarxien Temples*, p. 17.

53   Marija Gimbutas, *The Living Goddesses*, Berkeley, CA: University of California Press, 2001, p. 97.

54   Francis X. Aloisio, *A Cosmic Perspective to the Maltese Temples: An Alternative Handbook & Guide*, 2019, p. 99.

55   Cheryl Straffon, "The Goddess in the Temple," Part 1, ND.

56   Anthony Bonanno, *The Archaeology of Malta & Gozo*, p. 50.

57   Anthony Bonanno, *The Archaeology of Malta & Gozo*, p. 52.

58   Sharon Sultana, *The National Museum of Archaeology—The Neolithic Period*, Malta: Heritage Books, 2010, p. 38.

59   Klaus Albrecht, *Malta's Temples*.

60   Lenie Reedijk, *Sirius*.

61   Lenie Reedijk, *Sirius*, pp. 147-150.

62   Katya Stroud, *Ħaġar Qim & Mnajdra Prehistoric Temples—Qrendi*, Malta: Heritage Books, 2010.

63   Katya Stroud, *Ħaġar Qim & Mnajdra*, p. 43.

64   Katya Stroud, *Ħaġar Qim & Mnajdra*, p. 27.

65   quoted in Tore Lomsdalen, *Sky and Purpose in Prehistoric Malta,* p. 40.

66   Tore Lomsdalen, *Sky and Purpose in Prehistoric Malta*, p. xxi.

67   David H. Trump, *Malta Prehistory*, p. 151.

68   Tore Lomsdalen, *Sky and Purpose in Prehistoric Malta*.

69   Tore Lomsdalen, *Sky and Purpose in Prehistoric Malta*, p. 143.

70   See Tore Lomsdalen, *Sky and Purpose in Prehistoric Malta*, pp. 122–127; Katya Stroud, *Ħaġar Qim & Mnajdra*

Prehistoric Temples, p. 42; Anthony Bonanno, *The Archaeology of Malta & Gozo*, p. 40; and exhibits in the Visitor Center.

71   Klaus Albrecht, *Malta's Temples*, p. 79.

72   Lenie Reedijk, *Sirius*, p. 126.

73   Tore Lomsdalen, *Sky and Purpose in Prehistoric Malta*, p. xxi.

74   Klaus Albrecht, *Malta's Temples*, p. 61.

75   Lenie Reedijk, *Sirius*, p. 141.

76   Tore Lomsdalen, *Sky and Purpose in Prehistoric Malta*, pp. 152-153.

77   Mifsud et al., *Malta—Echoes of Plato's Island*, 2nd revised edition.

78   Mifsud et al., *Malta—Echoes of Plato's Island*, p. 42.

79   Francis X. Aloisio, *A Cosmic Perspective to the Maltese Temples*, p. 95.

80   Francis X. Aloisio, *An Alternative Handbook to the Maltese Temples—A Cosmic Perspective & Guide*, Malta: Culture33sixty, 2012, p. 13.

81   Francis X. Aloisio, *An Alternative Handbook*, p. 17.

82   Francis X. Aloisio, *An Alternative Handbook*, p. 18.

83   Francis X. Aloisio, *An Alternative Handbook*, p. 22.

84   Lenie Reedijk, *Sirius*, p. 122.

85   Francis X. Aloisio, private communication, 9 June 2019.

86   Graham Hancock, *Underworld*.

87   Anton Mifsud et al., *Malta—Echoes of Plato's Island.*

88   Graham Hancock, *Underworld.*

89   Freddy Silva, *The Missing Lands—Uncovering Earth's Pre-Flood Civilization*, Invisible Temple, 2019, p. 176.

90   Freddy Silva, *The Missing Lands*, p. 177.

91   Tore Lomsdalen, *Sky and Purpose in Prehistoric Malta*, p. xviii.

92   Tore Lomsdalen, *Sky and Purpose in Prehistoric Malta*, p. xix.

93   David H. Trump, *Malta Prehistory*, p. 199.

94   Katya Stroud, *Ħaġar Qim & Mnajdra*, p. 43.

95   Anthony Bonanno, *The Archaeology of Malta & Gozo*, p. 71; David H. Trump, *Malta Prehistory*, p. 199; and Katya Stroud, *Ħaġar Qim & Mnajdra*, p. 42.

96   Tore Lomsdalen, *Sky and Purpose in Prehistoric Malta*, pp. 82–84.

97   see Tore Lomsdalen *Sky and Purpose in Prehistoric Malta*, and Lenie Reedijk, *Sirius*, for a discussion of the "how."

98   Lenie Reedijk, *Sirius*, pp. 103–105.

99   Tore Lomsdalen, *Sky and Purpose in Prehistoric Malta*, p. xx.

100   Tore Lomsdalen, *Sky and Purpose in Prehistoric Malta.*

101   Freddy Silva, *The Missing Lands.*

102   Lenie Reedijk, *Sirius.*

103   Klaus Albrecht, *Malta's Temples*.

104   Tore Lomsdalen, *Sky and Purpose in Prehistoric Malta*.

105   see Marija Gimbutas, *The Living Goddesses*.

106   see, for example, Lucy Goodison and Christine Morris, editors, *Ancient Goddesses—The Myths and the Evidence*, London: British Museum Press, 1998.

107   T. Eric Peet, *Rough Stone Monuments and Their Builders*, p. 168, and pp. 175–176.

108   see Marija Gimbutas, *The Living Goddesses*, p. 220, note 9.

109   re Steatopygia, see http://humanphenotypes.net/metrics/steatopygia.html

110   David H. Trump, *Malta Archaeology*, p. 25.

111   David H. Trump, *Malta Prehistory*, p. 112.

112   David H. Trump, *Malta Prehistory*, p. 94.

113   Cheryl Straffon, "The Goddess in the Temple," Part 1, ND.

114   David H. Trump, *Malta Prehistory*, p. 113.

115   Jean Hani, *The Symbolism of the Christian Temple*, San Raphael, CA: Sophia Perennis, English translation, 2007.

116   David H. Trump, *Cart-Ruts and their Impact on the Maltese Landscape*, Malta: Heritage Books, 2008, includes a complete gazetteer.

117   David H. Trump, *Cart-Ruts*, p. 3.

118   Anthony Bonanno, *The Archaeology of Malta & Gozo*, p. 85.

119   David H. Trump, *Cart-Ruts*, p. 11.

120   David H. Trump, *Cart-Ruts*, p. 13.

121   D. N. Mottershead et al., "The Cart Ruts of Malta: An Applied Geomorphology Approach," *Antiquity* 82: 2008.

122   Antonio Arnaiz-Villena et al., "Malta and Lanzarote (Canary Islands, Spain) Cart-ruts and Rock Prehistoric Calendar at Zonzamas, Lanzarote," *Int. J. Mod. Anthrop.*, 2018, p. 16.

123   David H. Trump, *Cart-Ruts*, p. 21.

124   Anthony Bonanno, *The Archaeology of Malta & Gozo*, p. 84.

125   Anthony Bonanno, *The Archaeology of Malta & Gozo*, p. 84.

126   Anthony Bonanno, *The Archaeology of Malta & Gozo*, p. 85.

127   Claudia Sagona, *The Archaeology of Malta from the Neolithic through the Roman Period*. New York: Cambridge University Press, 2015.

128   Francis X. Aloisio, *A Cosmic Perspective to the Maltese Temples*, p. 92.

129   Francis X. Aloisio, *A Cosmic Perspective to the Maltese Temples*, p. 93.

130   Francis X. Aloisio, *A Cosmic Perspective to the Maltese Temples*, p. 94.

131   Erich von Däniken, quoted in http://www.cartrutsmalta.com/category/cart-ruts-mystery/.

132   see Marina Warner, *Alone of All Her Sex—The Myth and Cult of the Virgin Mary*, London: Vintage Press 2000 (original copyright 1976).

133   Francis X. Aloisio, private communication, 2013.

134   Francis X. Aloisio, *A Cosmic Perspective to the Maltese Temples*, pp. 147–148.

135   Francis X. Aloisio, *A Cosmic Perspective to the Maltese Temples*, pp. 135–6.

136   Francis X. Aloisio, private communication, 2013.

137   see Marina Warner, *Alone of All Her Sex—The Myth and Cult of the Virgin Mary*, for extensive discussions of this topic.

Bibliography

Albrecht, Klaus. *Malta's Temples—Alignments and Religious Motives*. 2nd Edition in English. Potsam: Sven Nather Verlag, 2007; first published in German, 2001.

Aloisio, Francis Xavier. *A Cosmic Perspective to the Maltese Temples: An Alternative Handbook & Guide*. 3rd, renamed, and expanded edition of An Alternative Handbook (2012, 2014). Francis Xavier Aloisio, MaltaTempleJourneys: e-book, 2019.

Aloisio, Francis Xavier. *An Alternative Handbook to the Maltese Temples—A Cosmic Perspective & Guide*. Malta: Culture3sixty, 2012.

Aloisio, Francis Xavier. *Islands of Dream: The Temples of Malta—Hidden Mysteries Revealed*. Booklocker.com: 2011. (Aloisio has written other books on the same theme, including Islands of Dream Speak, a compilation of travelers' accounts, research, etc. Check the internet.)

Archaeo-acoustical Hertz information from https://mysteriousuniverse.org/2018/08/the-mysterious-catacombs-of-malta/.

Arnaiz-Villena, Antonio, Marcial Medina, Jose Palacio-Gruber, Adrián Lopez-Nares and Valentín Ruiz-del-Valle. "Malta and Lanzarote (Canary Islands, Spain) Cart-ruts and Rock Prehistoric Calendar at Zonzamas, Lanzarote - 'Quesera'/Cheeseboard-," *International Journal of Modern Anthropology (Int. J. Mod. Anthrop.)* (2018) Vol: 2, Issue No: 11, pp. 214–231.

Bonanno, Anthony. *The Archaeology of Malta & Gozo—5000 BC–AD 1091*. Heritage Malta, 2017.

Brown, Elizabeth. *Dowsing – The Ultimate Guide for the 21st Century*. London: Hay House, 2010.

Cart-ruts: http://www.cartrutsmalta.com/.

Däniken, Erich von. *Signs of the Gods*, quoted in http://www.cartrutsmalta.com/category/cart-ruts-mystery/.

Debertolis, Paolo, and Niccolò Bisconti. "Archaeoacoustical analysis and ceremonial customs in an ancient hypogeum," Sociology Study, Vol. 3, No. 10: 803-814, October 2013. http://www.sbresearchgroup.eu/index.php/en/research-papers/199-archaeoacoustics-analysis-and-ceremonial-customs-in-an-ancient-hypogeum.

Di Cesare, Vittorio, and Adriano Forgione. "The Skulls of the Mother Goddess," HERA Magazine. https://www.bibliotecapleyades.net/arqueologia/esp_malta04.htm.

Elongated heads: Melanie Drury. "Why are these elongated skulls at Ħal Saflieni Hypogeum shrouded in mystery?" 21 January 2019, https://www.guidememalta.com/en/why-are-these-elongated-skulls-at-hal-saflieni-hypogeum-shrouded-in-mystery.

Fabri, Nadia. *Għar Dalam—The Cave, The Museum, and the Garden—Birzebbuga*. Malta Insight Heritage Guides. Malta: Heritage Books, 2007.

Għar Dalam: See https://www.timesofmalta.com/articles/view/20050320/letters/palaeolithic-man-in-malta.95701 for other finds at Għar Dalam that may have been much earlier than 5900 BCE.

Gimbutas, Marija. *The Living Goddesses*. Edited and supplemented by Mariam Robbins Dexter. Berkeley, CA: University of California Press, 1999; paperback edition, 2001.

Goodison, Lucy, and Christine Morris, editors. *Ancient Goddesses—The Myths and the Evidence*. London: British Museum Press, 1998.

Hancock, Graham. *Underworld—The Mysterious Origins of Civilization.* One section is devoted to Malta. New York: Three Rivers Press, 2003.

Hani, Jean. *The Symbolism of the Christian Temple.* First published in French, 1978. San Rafael, CA: Sophia Perennis, English translation, 2007.

Jessop, Lois. "Malta, Entrance to the Cavern World." *Journal of Borderland Research,* vol. 17, No. 2. (https://borderland-sciences.org/journal/vol/17/n02/Jessop_Malta_Cavern_World.html).

Keith, Arthur. "Discovery of Neanderthal Man in Malta, "1918, *Nature,* 101, 404-405.

Lomsdalen, Tore. *Sky and Purpose in Prehistoric Malta: Sun, Moon, and Stars at the Temples of Mnajdra.* Ceredigion, Wales: Sophia Centre Press, University of Wales, 2014.

Malone, Caroline, research: sources include https://www.timesofmalta.com/articles/view/20180316/life-features/700-years-added-to-maltas-history.673498.

Mifsud, Anton. Times of Malta interview, 2016, https://www.timesofmalta.com/articles/view/20160619/local/could-the-first-maltese-have-been-neanderthals.615901.

Mifsud, Anton, and Simon Mifsud. *Dossier Malta—Evidence for the Magdalenian.* Malta: Proprint Company Ltd., 1997. (See pp. 168–173 for a discussion of the Hypogeum; pp. 173–179 for a discussion on Għar Hasan.)

Mifsud, Anton, Simon Mifsud, Chris Agius Sultana, and Charles Savona-Ventura. *Malta—Echoes of Plato's Island,* 2nd revised edition. Malta: The Prehistoric Society of Malta, 2001.

Mifsud, Anton, and Charles Savona-Ventura, editors. *Facets of Maltese Prehistory*. Malta: Prehistoric Society of Malta, 1999.

Missing Children in the Hypogeum and Lois Jessop article: Melanie Drury. "Stranger Things: The Mystery of the Lost Children of Ħal Saflieni Hypogeum, 14 January 2019, https://www.guidememalta.com/en/stranger-things-the-mystery-of-the-lost-children-of-hal-saflieni-hypogeum.

Mottershead, D. N., Alastair Pearson, and Martin Schaefer. "The Cart Ruts of Malta: An Applied Geomorphology Approach," *Antiquity* 82: 1065–1079.

Pace, Anthony. *The Ħal Saflieni Hypogeum—Paola*. Malta Insight Heritage Guides. Malta: Heritage Books, 2004.

Pace, Anthony. *The Tarxien Temples—Tarxien*. Malta Insight Heritage Guides. Malta: Heritage Books, 2010.

Peet, T. Eric. *Rough Stone Monuments and Their Builders*, London and New York: Harper & Brothers, 1912.

Reedijk, Lenie. *Sirius—The Star of the Maltese Temples*. The Netherlands: Malet Books, 2018.

Sagona, Claudia. *The Archaeology of Malta from the Neolithic through the Roman Period*. New York: Cambridge University Press, 2015.

Sant Caruana, Daphne M. *Ġgantija Temples and Heritage Park—Xagħra, Gozo*. Malta Insight Heritage Guides. Malta: Heritage Books, 2015.

Savona-Ventura, Charles, and Anton Mifsud. *Hasan's Cave—Geology, Folklore and Antiquities*. Malta: Heritage Books, 2000.

Silva, Freddy. *The Missing Lands—Uncovering Earth's Pre-Flood Civilization*. Invisible Temple: 2019.

Steatopygia: http://humanphenotypes.net/metrics/steato-pygia.html.

Straffon, Cheryl. "The Goddess in the Temple: Life, Death & Rebirth at Maltese Temple Sites" Part 1, https://www.goddess-pages.co.uk/galive/issue-17-home/the-goddess-in-the-temple-2/.

Stroud, Katya. *Ħaġar Qim & Mnajdra Prehistoric Temples—Qrendi. Malta Insight Heritage Guides*. Malta: Heritage Books, 2010.

Sultana, Sharon. *The National Museum of Archaeology—The Neolithic Period*. Malta Insight Heritage Guides. Malta: Heritage Books, 2010.

Trump, David (D. H.). *Malta: An Archaeological Guide*. London: Faber & Faber Ltd., 1972.

Trump, David H. *Malta Prehistory and Temples*. 3rd Edition. Malta: Midsea Books Ltd., Heritage Malta, 2008.

Trump, David H. *Cart-Ruts and Their Impact on the Maltese Landscape. Malta Insight Heritage Guides*. Malta: Heritage Books, 2008.

Warner, Marina. *Alone of All Her Sex—the Myth and Cult of the Virgin Mary*. London: Vintage Press, 2000 (original copyright 1976).

Index

A

Agape tables 160

animal relief carvings 87

articulated skeletons 52

astronomical alignments vi, 4, 80, 93, 101, *104, 107,* 184

astronomical events 31, 92, 106, 109, 112, 131

Atlantis 74, 115, 116, 139

B

BLESSING 6

boat graffiti 87

Bronze Age 14, 15, 35, 81, 87, *89,* 134–139, 164, 192

bull fresco 72

bulls 61, 72, 85, 104

C

Calypso vii, ix, 141–144

Caravaggio 156, 158

Cart-ruts ix, 205, 207, 208

cataclysm 70, 115

Catacombs ix, 61, 158–165, 176

Clapham Junction ix, 132, 134, 138

L

M

N

O

T

Ta' Ḥaġrat Temples ix, 33, 36, 39, 41

Ta' Pinu Basilica ix, 147

Tarxien Phase 35, 102, 113, 190

Tarxien Temples ix, 49, 58, 68, 80, 81, 87–90, 92, 120, 197, 200, 210

taurodontism 20

teeth 20, 22, 24–27, 184

telluric energies 118, 195

Temple Period 13, 14, 34, 81, 94, 119, 134, 176, 190

torba 35, 84, 104

Tree of Life 64

U

UNESCO 13, 30, 33, 36, 41, 58, 80, 93

V

Venus of Ḥaġar Qim 99, 125, 128

Virgin Mary 147, 148, 152, 157, 165, 167, 168, 174, 179, 193, 206, 211

votive offerings 150, 177, 178

W

Winter Solstice Sunrise 41, 106, 113

X

Y

About the Authors

Elyn Aviva, Ph.D. (Princeton University, Cultural Anthropology; dissertation on the modern-day Camino de Santiago in Spain); Master's in Divinity (Iliff School of Theology); ordained minister (Church of Universal Worship); award-winning fiber artist. Other books include *Following the Milky Way*, 2nd edition, *Where Heaven and Earth Unite*, *The Question: A Magical Fable*, and the *Powerful Places Guidebook* series. For more information, go to www.pilgrimsprocess.com, www.powerfulplaces.com, www.fiberalchemy.com, and Facebook Elyn Aviva Writes.

Gary C. White, Ph.D., Distinguished Professor Emeritus, Iowa State University. Award-winning composer and author of numerous music theory and composition textbooks. He has studied dowsing and geomancy with Sig Lonegren, Dominique Susani, and Ferran Blasco. White is co-author of the *Powerful Places Guidebook* series and production director for Pilgrims Process Publishers. For more information, go to www.pilgrimsprocess.com and www.powerfulplaces.com.

www.ingramcontent.com/pod-product-compliance
Lightning Source LLC
Chambersburg PA
CBHW022130050726
47590CB00002B/490